MAKE 'EM LAUGH

MAKE 'EM LAUGH

Life Studies of Comedy Writers

by

William F. Fry, M.D. and Melanie Allen, Ph.D.

Science and Behavior Books, Inc. • Palo Alto, California

Typeset by Vera Allen Composition Service,
Castro Valley, California

Library of Congress Catalog Card Number 75-23593

ISBN 0-8314-0041-2

To our families—both immediate and extended—with our heartfelt thanks for their assistance and support.

Also, in completing this book, Melanie realized the influence of her grandmother, Sadie Fagen, who taught her that every moment of tragedy can end with a laugh

---

A Word to the Reader . . .

What follows in this book are seven life study interviews with some of the most successful comedy writers in Hollywood. Also in this book is the attempt of the authors to place these interviews into focus—a focus representing the point of view of a new, positive kind of psychology. Humor and creativity have always been appreciated, but seldom understood. What Doctors Fry and Allen offer here could be the most active effort in understanding these two elusive subjects since the enormous contributions of Sigmund Freud.

There is another dimension to the significance of these—and other—comedy writers. In this country alone a daily average of forty million people watch television and are affected by what these people write. Television is fun. It has enormous potential to increase our ability to identify with one another. These creators of comedy can be said to be among the most important and influential people in this country. They have the power to change attitudes and create new images.

Robert S. Spitzer, M.D.
Editor-in-Chief

Contents

Acknowledgments

Preparation of this book, reporting our extensive studies of humor and creativity, has required the assistance and cooperation of many people. We wish to acknowledge our indebtedness to these persons for their enthusiastic contributions, their hospitality, and their warm encouragement.

Foremost, of course, we are deeply indebted to the talented and richly human comedy writers who have shared so much of themselves with us and with the world. Needless to say, our studies would not exist without their fundamental assistance. We also wish to emphasize that this study could have been quite a different experience if our subjects had been of a different attitude. Their responsiveness and their sincere and vivacious participation made our experiences with them not only enlightening and fruitful, but also extremely enjoyable.

We wish to express our deep gratitude to all those who acted for us in arranging the interviews, in introducing us to the writers, in lightening the burden of practical and technical details related to the actual interviewing. These benefactors include James McLaughlin Smith, Ron Mardigian, and Marian Rees.

A truly heroic job at the tape recorder and typewriter must not go unrecognized. The interviews were live-taped, and a shorthand record was taken by Mrs. Elizabeth S. Fry—no mean feat in itself, considering the interview durations, their rapid-fire character, and the wide range of topics covered. The tapes were then transcribed. Anyone familiar with tape transcription knows the great difficulties involved in this task. Add to these "ordinary" difficulties the vitality, forcefulness, enthusiasm, and complexity of the writers' discourse, and one can understand why this job was "heroic." Mrs. Katherine Smith was the star who performed so skillfully and patiently on most of the transcription. The task was completed with no less skill by Mr. Gene Belote.

Our particular appreciation is extended to Mrs. Frances Lear, who was of special assistance with the initial editing of the Norman Lear interview. It was Mrs. Lear who first envisioned this material in book form.

We also want to express our gratitude to Ms. Jacqueline Oberman and Mrs. Teresa Wu for their loyal typing enterprise.

Dr. Peter Ostwald, of the Langley Porter Institute in San Francisco provided invaluable technical assistance.

There has been a real familial warmth in the preparation of this book. This warmth has been infinitely enhanced by the nurturance of our talented editor, Peggy Granger, and our innovative publisher, Bob Spitzer.

Melanie Allen   William Fry, Jr.
Los Angeles, California   Portola Valley, California
September, 1975   September, 1975

A Historical Foreword

Any study of human experience has, as a natural back-drop, the panorama of human desire and human expression. This book focuses basically on two human experiences: humor and creativity, and on their union in the creating *of* humor. By venturing into the study of these phenomena, we are also entering into an inquiry regarding human motivation in general. In other words, we are not just asking: "What makes the creator want to express himself in humorous terms?" but are implicitly involved in seeking an answer to broader questions such as: "What makes us move?" or "What moves us in this human life?"

Thinkers have struggled over this issue since the time of ancient Greeks. We thought it fitting to present a brief history of how man has viewed himself through history, particularly as it pertains to humor and to creativity. Many of you may choose to enter directly into the life studies without going on this brief trip with us, but we offer our own bias—that this brief review will help you to lay a groundwork for more meaningful connection with the lives of the people featured in this book. We feel that all of us can better put into perspective the points of view represented by the comedy writers, having the historical context as a frame of reference.

From early times, especially in the work of British empiricists such as Thomas Hobbes, man has been frequently pictured as a rather savage creature who is, at root, egoistic and, if left alone, would choose to gorge himself with the goods of life, no matter whose pocket he had to pick. In *The Leviathan,* Hobbes proposed that societies were necessary in order to control, through group pressure, the base instincts of individuals.

This conception of man and woman untamed and seeking pleasure and the fulfillment of basic needs with little attendance to others became known as *egoism* or *hedonism* and came, in time, to serve as the bases for the psychoanalytic theories of Sigmund Freud and the behavioristic theories of John Watson, B. F. Skinner, and others. Although both of these psychological schools speak in different languages, the *leitmotif* within is the same: All motivation can be traced to the drive to reduce *pain,* thereby giving us that release referred to as *pleasure.*

This idea of release was somehow involved in the thinking of other theorists focussing on human emotion. Humor was treated with this in mind. At the turn of the century, Darwin, for instance, in his discussions of the role of emotion, pegged humor as an adaptive mechanism, feeling that it was most possibly a refinement of some primitive impulse that restores us to equilibrium after conditions of danger or distress. Hayworth described laughter as a basic signal denoting the return of the tribe to safety.

Out of this heritage, there arose a small group of humor researchers whom we could call release theorists. They speculated that the organism gets rid of unnecessary or excess energy in the form of laughter.

Spencer, for instance, believed that the most natural course of expression for this excess energy was via the organs utilized for speech and the same muscles used in respiration. Bliss and Gregory, writing in the early 20th century, presented the idea that all humor experiences represent the sudden release of repressed materials. As we shall see in the first chapter of this book, these constructs definitely parallel Freud's theory of wit. Both Bliss and Gregory felt that man is at odds with the social order and that people build up tension if they are not able to express certain of their impulses. Gregory felt that the release of such tension in substitute form (such as a joke) provides instantaneous pleasure. Several other contemporary humor researchers (Dworkin & Efran; Levine; and Strickland) concur with Freud in believing that humor functions as an outlet for arousal states which have no *direct* arena for expression. The humor experience is substituted for direct manifestation of frustration or hostility.

Even though behaviorists also posit tension-reduction as a basic motive in human behavior, another group of contemporary humor theorists, led by Byrne, feel that people learn the *habit* of using humor as a successful coping mechanism. Those who have had success using humor in the past will tend to use it again.

Although Freud's theory and that of his advocates clearly involves the use of humor as a substitute and Byrne's approach seems more positive in that he is discussing successful coping rather than the defensive or subconscious use of humor, it will be clear to most of you that both approaches picture man against the elements, involved in some way in avoiding pain and obtaining pleasure.

A very different approach to human life was provided by such writers as Rousseau and Melville. In Rousseau's *Confessions* and in the pictures given us of natives by Melville, we are confronted with the "noble savage" genre. Both of these writers feel that man is basically good and that it is the society which is the corrupter. Left alone and unbridled, men and women are in their most perfect and "noble" state.

In the 20th century, a new school in psychology grew rapidly in the United States. Known as the "Third Force," leaders in this new school passionately objected to the pessimistic images of humankind provided by the Freudians and the behaviorists. They also denied that society is necessarily antagonistic to the expansion of the human being. They found, in other words, a *growth potential* inherent both in the individual *and* in the society. Leaders in this new school of humanistic psychology were from many disciplines. Among them were such prominent thinkers as Charlotte Bühler, Kurt Goldstein, S. I. Hayakawa, Abraham Maslow, Lewis Mumford, David Riesman, and Carl Rogers. The work of these thinkers was clearly reflective of a new *zeitgeist*, a "spirit of the time" when a positive and hopeful image of man emerged out of many disciplines simultaneously. Similarly, the movement of many adults and young people in that decade of The Sixties, was demonstrative of the feeling that human beings wanted to rebel against the growing alienation in modern existence. Like the humanistic psychologists, many people came to believe that only through the reconstruction of human life on a more intimate basis, wherein relationships with others and self-fulfillment were given primary priority, could people really live again as people rather than as empty automatons. Descartes wrote, *Cogito, ergo sum:* "I think, therefore I am." Camus, in confronting the absurdities of contemporary life, wrote, *J'aime, donc je suis:* "I love, therefore I am." He changed the spirit of Descartes' message out of a need to show his deep belief that, lest we live rich emotional lives, we do not really live at all.

To the humanistic psychologist, humor is a means of actualizing one's self while coping with life's ups and downs.

Is humor only a sudden explosion, a release from pain or uptightness? Or does humor emerge out of a growing wisdom, to resound in the air as a great, goat-cry of life, a triumphant transcendance? These questions, long-pondered, are at the heart of our inquiry.

Introduction

This book brings us into close, intimate touch with a type of magic. It is a magic of every-day. It is a magic of family life, of being on the job, of going to school, of bowling and golfing and tennis, of the backyard barbecue, of gathering outside the church after services, of shopping at the grocery, of teaching and learning, of Congress and sandlot baseball, of PTA and G.A.L. and Scouts, of plumbing and riveting and sweeping and cutting meat in the butcher shop, of bailing navel lint, of insurance offices, of marinas, of ski slopes, of gasoline stations, of doctor's waiting rooms, and standing in line at the hamburger stand, of threshing wheat and planting corn, of court rooms and beer halls, of children and parents and grandparents, of neighbors and friends. This is everyone's every-day magic.

It is humor.

The practitioners of this magic are universal alchemists. Prominent among them are the comedy writers—the people who invent the humor which stirs the mirth ready at the doorstep in all of us. Each day thousands of people all over the world use the humor inventions of comedy writers for making their livelihoods and getting their messages across. Each day hundreds of thousands—even millions—are entertained by these inventions, are given blessed moments of relief from ordinary and, sometimes, extraordinary cares. Peals of laughter that echo across the entire earth-globe are songs of tribute to the comedy writers' talents. They make rich contributions, indeed, to the lives of fellow humans.

1

In this book, seven of these writer-alchemist-magicians share portions of their private lives, their private thoughts, their creative and humorous experiences with us. Most previous studies of humor professionals have dealt with those who primarily *present* comedy—many extremely talented in their own right. These have included comedians, clowns, actors, jesters, satirists, buffoons, and mimes. Too long, the *inventors* of humor have been sequestered in the wings, as several of the writers reminisce, or in stuffy, hot little rooms where they are manacled to typewriters so that they will continue to pound out the material that makes the show go on. This book gives their profession time at stage center and offers perspective on their significance in our lives.

We, the authors, feel constrained to describe how we were led to correct that unfortunate neglect. The interviewing of these writers and this book are natural products of chains of events in our own individual lives, and are inevitable consequences of forces within us. We have considered that our sharing these personal matters will give the reader a better introduction to the writer-interviews which follow.

Melanie's Story

How did I come to study humor? How did I ever dare search behind the moments of spontaneous joy that come about when any of us laugh in the faces of the gods and goddesses, moments when we realize our own limitations as we realize theirs, simultaneously respecting our ability to transcend the ordinary and emerge godlike?

When I was kindergarten age, summer was long. I had friends, but they weren't always there. Arlene was; I could bring her to me just by making her be there. She was, I told my Mom, from "across the highway." There was one house in the woods across the highway in those days, and Arlene came out of that house whenever I wanted her. She got safely across the highway traffic and brought cookies. The war was being fought somewhere far away. Arlene and I collected little flags and talked about our people in the war. Her brother was a foot soldier and my Uncle Maurie was in the Navy. I would sing her the song about "Bell Bottom Trousers, coat of Navy blue," and tell her that my Uncle Maurie was the funniest man in the world. Nobody would ever be able to kill him. And I would make Arlene laugh just as I made my little sister Janice laugh, by tickling her in just the right place or coming at her with just the right funny face. We laughed right through the war and the war ended.

My own life, however, had just begun. It's been an amazing life, pushed all over the place by an intensity that sometimes scares other people and sometimes scares me. Its burning led me to try many things, so that I could feed it, ease its hunger, and equal its power.

I found that the burning was best satisfied and perpetuated by hearing the stories of others and becoming part of the lives of others. It took me a long time to understand strongly enough, clearly enough to act.

When I was sixteen and a student at the University of Minnesota, I wanted more than anything else in the world to play my clarinet—forever. For some years, I poured all of my burning into music. At the age of eighteen, I heard the echo of my horn in a world that was growing more devoid of people, and I left for UCLA where I became a film student. The rhythm was in me, but as I told my Grandpa (who wanted terribly for me to remain a musician) writing is a more natural language for me to express that rhythm. For several years, the intensity was invested solely in writing. I graduated from UCLA's Film School and went to Europe on a Fulbright in cinema writing.

When I came back I began work with two unusually talented young men who were doing movies at the time: Bud Yorkin and Norman Lear. They gave me a beautiful office in their suite and did all they could to help me adjust to an Industry that had no relationship to my childhood dreams of Hollywood. I sat in that beautiful, paneled office, trying out a language that had always been easy for me, only to find it going frozen. It was cold in the film industry in those days. People distanced themselves from other people in order to survive. When I found myself isolated, I left.

I needed to be with people and to make my life of that. In 1967, everything came together for me, and I returned to school to study psychology at Valley State College (now California State University at Northridge). During my second year, a fine teacher of mine, Patricia Keith-Spiegel, programmed what must have been one of the first university courses in humor in the United States. It was a great, uproarious experience. The whole class was like a vaudeville troupe. Everyone had his or her own style. Between making jokes and collecting jokes, we turned out research projects in humor. I really loved that course, because we were tapping unknown territory, exploring phenomena that could *not* be easily measured, but which could be worked with. We were challenged to expand our consciousness in order to be able to describe and explain such an elusive event as a moment's laughter.

During the time I was in the humor class, I concentrated on a study involving American middle-class housewives. I was interested in exploring how their levels of frustration and feelings of self-esteem and self-worth related to the kinds of humor they found most funny. Did highly frustrated women, for example, prefer cartoons in which male figures were obviously being ridiculed by hostile women?

While still at Valley State, I worked in the laboratory for several months trying to determine whether or not subjects, during humor experiences, could be said only to be reducing tension. My associates, Bill St. John and Cecile Goldfarb agreed with me that humor seemed to be tension-*increasing* as well as a tension-reduction experience. I liked laboratory work; I found it most satisfying for the clues it gave me in working with theoretical problems. But I was soon to return to my preference—field research. My interest in the physiology of humor continued.

Some of the students in the humor class were chosen by PKS, as we called her, to be part of a large Humor Symposium at the Western Psychological Association meetings of 1969. On that panel in Vancouver was a very scholarly but funny psychiatrist whom I spotted as also coming from "left field": Bill Fry. That was the birthplace of this project.

And, in the writing of this book, I discovered something else about my love of people. I found that most people I loved deeply lived with humor as a gift and as a major part of their lifestyles and vocabularies. They might use different styles, but the ensuing result was much the same. Both of my Grandpas, for example, had a terrific thing going with humorous nonsense games from the "Old Country." These little games combined wild words that defy spelling with neat rhythms to make my little sister and brother and me giggle our heads off. In one, Grandpa Abie began by counting off our fingers, saying, "Ettimo, ettimo, ettimo . . . Then, he'd begin moving up our arm with his hand, increasing the pace as he moved: Tut-pen, tut-colodda; tut-pen, tut-calodda—until he got to the end, moving swiftly into the pocket of our underarms and tickled us until we were hysterical.

Grandma Sadie's humor was distinctly different. She punctuated life with sudden, wise phrases that came off funny partly because of an Austrian twist to her oral and written words, but mostly because of her incredible timing. Uncle Maurie was my Dad's brother; the family rascal. He had a burly humor that was right out there, straight out there all the way—just as *he* was: gutsy, earthy, warm-male-bear-love-of-life, even through several heart attacks.

My mom—even the sound of her laugh is funny. And I am proud to say that people think I inherited that contagious, ridiculous laugh: ha *ha!* My dad's humor is in his eyes, just as are most of his feelings. I learned the power of my own wit through watching his eyes when I was a child, and seeing him try to keep a stern look while scolding me as I went through my numbers: grimaces, winks, and all, and finally seeing him fall apart, no longer able to be angry at his *enfant terrible.*

Others have made great contributions to my life with laughter as well. Norman and Frances Lear, who showed me the funniest dinner table scenes I'd ever experienced—so funny they cut through the long pain I experienced at the end of first love. Four teen-agers, Brian and Tina, who coped with growing up and with being flaming non-conformists by adept ad-libbing and great imitations; and Mike Weiss and Mike Tenner who coped by their boundless wit. And Ingrid, who has struggled on many fronts across the world to find her world, whose scars radiate beauty when she emerges suddenly out of peak stress using her different languages and different lives in matchless punning and *double entendre.*

All of you I have loved—and others with you—for your ability to transcend "heaviness," bouncing out of it with the impetus of a turned phrase, "adding time to your lives," as Norman Lear put it, and by doing so, adding time to my own.

And, in thinking of my own life, I know that I have most loved myself in just such moments. All my long downers came about at times I could not appreciate life's absurdities enough to laugh at them, and all the highs came when I used my own gift of humor to laugh at myself, and to turn a moment's absurdity into meaning.

William's Story

In 1953, I became a member of an unlikely group, joined together for participation in research of an even more unlikely nature. Ethnologist Gregory Bateson had been awarded a research grant by Chester Barnard, then head of the Rockefeller Foundation. Mr. Barnard had been impressed by the original, clear, and inspired thinking Gregory had demonstrated in his early book, *Naven.* He decided to encourage that brain by offering an opportunity for its unfettered exercise. If this story sounds too much like the Renaissance to be true, I can only affirm that a few events of this nature really did take place during that era of surging postwar ebullience.

The almost unbelievable title chosen by Gregory for his research was, "The Project for Study of the Paradoxes of Abstraction in Communication." Four of us were in this original venture: Gregory, psychologist Jay Haley, anthropologist John Weakland, and myself. I had received the following letter:

Dear Bill:

Dr. Martha Mac Donald has just mentioned to me that you were thinking of going into research after the end of your residency. I think she mentioned to you that I expect to be building up a small research unit here in the Fall. My plan is to try to collect material demonstrating the role played by the Russellien paradoxes in psychotherapy.

If this might interest you, get in touch with me and we will discuss it.

Yours sincerely,
Gregory

Within a few short weeks after settling into our program, Gregory produced a list of elements of human and animal behavior, which he proposed to serve as a master study list. Each was to make selections from this list for preliminary investigation, with the intent of moving along these individual routes toward the central area of paradox research. Among the esoterics on that list were Zen Buddhism, hypnosis, play, schizophrenia, pagentry and ritual, humor, drama, psychotherapy, and metaphor.

While it seemed natural that I should apply myself to those subjects with which I had the most concentrated recent contact—schizophrenia and psychotherapy—I deliberately chose to avoid research commitment to those subjects because of my belief that a mixed exposure in my career would benefit both the clinical and research sides of my activities. Orientation limited to one direction, I reasoned, would result in my becoming a very well-informed specialist, but also a narrow-minded and impoverished pedant.

"Drama" had special appeal. I had enjoyed amateur theatrical activity during adolescence, and there is truth in the old saw about grease paint getting into your blood.

Also, "metaphor" attracted me. Writing poetry has been a hobby for years. There is little else of human behavior in which metaphor is more deliberately involved than in poetry. I believe that the capacity for metaphoric thought is one of the few most basic cerebral functions of at least mammalian life. Parenthetically, it is probably that basic function least recognized and regarded for its crucial contributions to making life what it is. Most people think of metaphor only in terms of its most explicit presence—that is, as a device in literature, as in poetry.

As attractive as these two fields appeared, many reasons converged onto my choice of humor as my steppingstone into the research core. I have always enjoyed humor immensely, being quick to laughter and susceptible to intense paroxysms of mirth—sometimes to the embarrassment of my loved ones. Telling jokes and engaging in humorous repartee are very pleasurable to me. Humor in the various entertainment and recreational media has invariably attracted me more vigorously than most other modes.

Humor was a powerfully unifying theme in my three-generation childhood family. My father, his father, and I—the one son—found humor to afford a reliable and ready path through the thicket of our often disparate desires. And our humor was always facilitated by input from the fourth male of the household—Joe Carter: butler, gardener, blithe spirit, who related to each of us with equal joviality. Laughter and jesting have also been touchstones in the family marriages, for my parents and my grandparents. My wife and I carry on the tradition and really treasure our moments of shared mirth.

These and others were reasons which sent me unself-consciously into a year-long study of the available humor literature. And it turned out, as is the case with quicksand and tapioca, that the more I read, the more involved I became. What had started as a preliminary investigation quickly became a lifetime research program.

I soon found that the humanities offered more statements about humor than did science, and even here much was speculation and suggestion, with few attempts to bring together the various viewpoints into at least a more orderly confusion. I also discovered that reading about humor continuously stimulated me to new thoughts on the subject. I would read a bit, and then think a lot, read a little more and then think a great deal more. The year was barely long enough to get through the more important books and articles, but I filled several notebooks with my musings and "strokes of genius." I concluded that humor offered a splendid opportunity for significant pioneering work. And I decided that I have a natural affinity for response to the subject.

The material bulging my notebooks rapidly became recognizable as the guts of a book. That book, *Sweet Madness—A Study of Humor* was completed in 1959 and published in 1963. The Bateson project terminated in 1962.

A grant from the National Institute of Mental Health, and the administrative support of the Mental Research Institute and its parent, the Palo Alto Medical Research Foundation, made it possible to explore humor areas needing further definitive research. I was joined in that exploration by linguist-anthropologist Edith Trager, then of San Jose State University, Calif., and Frances Underwood, anthropologist of the same institution. Dr. Trager originated the word "gelotology" from its Greek roots to designate "the science of laughter."

During 1963–64, I had the benefit of physiology consultation with neuro-psychiatrist Charles Yeager, at San Francisco's Langley Porter Institute. Our study led me to conclude that it would be desirable to establish a broader knowledge of the physiology of mirth—both to advance our basic information but also to make it possible to develop a profile of mirth that could be used as an instrument in other scientific studies. A series of physiology studies followed, with the assistance of Paul Stoft, director of Hewlett Packard Electronics Research Laboratory, and Con Rader, research engineer at Spinco Division, Beckman Instruments.

The word got around in psychology circles that I was doing this crazy thing and Dr. Patricia Keith-Spiegel, psychologist at San Fernando Valley State College, decided to take a chance with her professional reputation by inviting me to present some of my material and ideas on a humor panel at the 1969 annual Western Psychological Association meeting in Vancouver, B.C. I exercised restraint and things did not go as wildly as Patti may have feared. However, there was a young psychology Ph.D. candidate on the panel who apparently saw what I had taken pains to hide by my carefully-measured words.

Together

Our first meeting was relaxed and comfortable for us both. Melanie suggested a joint effort on some physiology study some time in the future. On July 7, 1969, a letter from Melanie included, "I would very much like to compare notes with you in the future. Plan to be in San Francisco area some time around the end of July. Will you have 'anything going' at that time? . . . I really enjoyed meeting you, liked your delivery, and hope we can meet again. . . ."

That July meeting did not take place. In January, 1970, Melanie's former employer, Bud Yorkin, was working with an idea of setting up a Don Rickles "special" in which Rickles would interview a psychiatrist. Melanie suggested William as the psychiatrist. For various reasons, the project didn't work out. But, on January 27, 1970, William wrote, "As a future project, I'll mention this now that I realize you have connections in the entertainment industry—I want to create the opportunity of interviewing some gag writers (not realizing at that time the impropriety of that moniker, but soon to be set straight). These are people who really know what humor is . . . I may put the touch on you at some future date for some introductions."

Melanie answered that she was interested and thought she could be of some help in getting people to interview and in helping with the interviews herself. By the end of summer progress had been made.

William's letter of June, 1970, brought the correspondence and telephone conversations between the two into an apt summary. "We want to gather material on:

1. Creative process of making a joke—prior level of tension, construction span, attendant thought process, post-creation mood, dreaming or fantasying, degree of self-amusement during construction, nature and degree of use of feedback mechanisms.

2. Creator's background—outside character, humor preferences, life history pattern and early experiences, family humor, culture or specific modeling, contrast between professional and personal life in humor, first association with formal humorous writing.

3. Creator's perception of changing styles of humor over a period of his professional life.

4. Creator's philosophic position—concept of humor.

5. Creator's impression of regional and socio-economic level variations in sense of humor.

6. Creator's viewpoints on dialect and its role in humor. There are various ways in which dialect contributes directly to the joke—in those cases where the joke depends on a stereotype about a certain type of person designated by the dialect. However, there are a great many jokes in which the dialect contributes indirectly. These latter jokes are funnier if done in dialect.

7. What emotions are to be avoided in joke content leading up to a punchline? Which ones would be antithetical to the generation of humor?

8. Creator's experience and judgment about various techniques of humor—rules of timing, word or sound sequence rules, 'funny' words or letters or sounds or numbers, punchline placement, joke complexity (multiple jokes), gag-to-gag continuity.

We should not put a great deal of pressure on ourselves, that this has to be done all at once. On the other hand, there's no point in being timid, in not diving right in and having a good time with it."

And that's exactly what we did.

Norman Lear

Humor and its Role in the Processes of Creativity and Life

NORMAN LEAR was born in 1922 in New Haven, Connecticut. His brief and hilarious career as a door-to-door salesman ended abruptly when he made his first sale of comedy material to Danny Thomas. His next big professional job was as co-writer of the Ford Star Revue and he was on his way. His hobbies are "tennis, music, art, literature, etc." (he added in his letter that there was a lot of "etc.").

His twenty-five year career in show business has accorded him much success, international recognition, and honors from both the film and television industry. A partial listing of his credits is listed below.

As a writer he wrote the screenplay for "Divorce, American Style," which gained an Academy Award nomination for him. Together with Bud Yorkin he created and produced television specials including "Another Evening with Fred Astaire," "Bobby Darin and Friends," "Henry Fonda and Family," "An Evening with Carol Channing," and "The Many Sides of Don Rickles."

He developed and produced "All in the Family," "Maude," "Sanford and Son," "Good Times," "The Jeffersons," and "Hot L Baltimore."

On the afternoon Norman Lear talked with us about his feelings at the "peak" of the creative process, when the "juices are flowing," the well-known producer/writer/media-innovator said, "Sometimes I can get carried away by the whole thing. I can get carried away completely. And *I can add time to my own life.*" (Authors' italics.)

A simple statement, seemingly, but to us, a complex and dramatic one. Through these few words, delivered spontaneously and with great intensity, we felt that Norman was expressing the entire meaning of the creative process for *him*—that the act of creativity is life-giving.

But what exactly makes the creative act so potent, so fecund for Norman? What gives him this sudden surge of invulnerability, this sense of self-transcendance? What makes him feel, for that moment, *that he can add time to his own life?*

We wager that if we knew the answer, we would unlock the door not only to the power of creativity or of humor, but to the still-unanswered puzzle of the role of motivation and emotions. As we described in our brief historical foreword, since ancient times, thinkers have debated these issues.

In contemporary psychology, personality theories are characterized by two basic images of man. The first is that held by psychoanalytically and behavioristically-oriented psychologists. They view man as a biological creature whose life is determined by past events, or by cause and effect relationships. Further, as we mentioned in the historical notes, they believe that all motivation centers in the desire to reduce tension and thereby gain pleasure.

Although Freudians and behaviorists use different jargon to sketch their theories, the basic message is the same: men and women are biologically-motivated, geared basically to removing tissue deficiencies. As we grow and develop, various other activities become associated with reduction of tissue needs and acquire their own power. They become (although they are secondary needs) functionally autonomous, and have the power to arouse us, to make us feel tense and uncomfortable (if we do *not* have them), or to make us feel satisfied. Among these secondary needs are the needs for relationships, for money, for status, for good grades, etc.

The reader will quickly understand that this manner of thinking reduces all human behavior to a reward-and-punishment-premise and to fixed cause-and-effect relationships.

This pessimistic picture of human life has been challenged by a rapidly-growing "third force" which has come to be known as humanistic psychology. As early as the thirties, Charlotte Bühler did her classic studies on babies in their first year of life. She observed infants in their cribs; dry, fed, and rested, and saw that they were playing with their fingers, exploring their little worlds—in short, increasing tension. Together with Kurt Goldstein and Abraham Maslow, she believed that explaining human existence solely in terms of tension-reduction was too simplistic; that there were many aspects of life too complex for such an explanation, particularly the thinking and action involved in such processes as exploration, curiosity, and creativity.

No responsible thinker in humanistic psychology denies that many of our actions take place out of the need for pleasure or the avoidance of pain. But, these psychologists recognize another motive basic to human life: the need to grow, to be further integrated—*the desire for self-fulfillment*, as Kurt Goldstein called it.

Maslow called this positive force, "growth motivation," admitting that not all human beings strive for such a state. Sometimes we are taken up with more primal needs (such as hunger or survival). Charlotte Bühler saw also that society often lent stimulation and opportunities for expansion in a positive way.

Clearly the tension-reduction schools of Freudianism and behavioristic psychology view humor and its purpose in a manner far different from the humanistic psychologists.

A life like Norman Lear's allows us to look closely at the development of one person and come to our own conclusions about his basic motivation. Is there a purpose beyond that of tension-reduction operative in Norman while he creates?

Exploration of the relationship between these psychological principles and the experiences of humor and of creativity was a prime motivation for our study, leading us into the arena of probing into the course of human lives. Incidentally, entering into such areas is often considered "soft" research by experimental scientists. Save for the laugh, smile, smirk, or the joke itself, one certainly cannot *see* or *hear* the creative process. Both of us, at one time or another, have engaged in "hard" experimental approaches to the study of humor. Fry wired up people to measure their laughter on print-outs, and recorded the laughter of humans, gorillas, and chimpanzees. He has also photographed their smiles, smirks, and grimaces. Allen spent one year of weekends locked up in a laboratory with human volunteers and a polygraph, telling subjects anxiety-provoking stories, and then observing whether or not the volunteers, under this stress, experienced reduction of tension through the subsequent viewing of cartoons. Despite high humor ratings given to cartoons by many of these stressed subjects, many of them showed an *increase* of tension during the presumed experience of humor.

In any event, we finally concluded that these experiments just weren't productive enough. So we unwired our gorillas and people and took up a different mode of research which resulted in this book.

Norman Lear proved to be an excellent subject for our work because of several factors. First of all, he has an excellent memory, and was able to recapture the events of childhood and young manhood with exquisite, vital detail. Equally important was his psychological orientation. He truly worked with us as "part of the team," seeming to fully understand the significance of certain events in the interaction of a family and the development of a child.

This was especially important to us, because we were interested in looking beyond the product to focus on the process. We wanted to learn how the writers became humorous in the first place, and how they use humor in their lives. We wanted to know whether or not they consciously deliberated or plan "being funny." We wondered how they reacted if given the applause or rewards of significant others during their youth, and how various factors related to their becoming producers and writers of humor in adult life.

Previous to this study, we already had begun to see as possibly distinct from one another, the act of laughing, other participatory experiences involving mirth, and the actual engagement of the subject in the creation of humor. We felt, obviously, that the best source of data on each life would be the writer himself.

We were especially impressed with the material Norman Lear provided us on the creative process. Since our interviews, Norman has been a sought-after person, because of the building of a television empire, following the success of "All in the Family." Interviews with him that followed have delved into many aspects of his life. However, none of them seems attuned to "Norman the creator at the typewriter." And, we feel this is true about much of the material written about artists. The concentration is on product or content, rather than the more elusive *process*.

Just what is the nature of the creative process? Is there any way of tapping the essence of those magical moments when the Muse sits upon the shoulder of the writer and seems to illuminate him? Or can we learn what it is like when the artist has been abondoned by the Muse and faces emptiness within and without?

The work of one author in particular is helpful in answering these questions. In *The Act of Creation*, Arthur Koestler delineated three domains of creativity.

His delineation allow us to integrate beautifully the analytic behavioristic conceptions of humor while giving credence to the perspective of the humanistic psychologists at the same time. Koestler's work supports our impression that humor-inventing and humor-discovering may be distinctly different, even for the same individual. When you enter into Norman Lear's domain of creativity, we think you will be able to see evidence of these different experiences.

Koestler borrows a term from Brennig James—the *ha ha* experience. As he describes it, this experience is an emotional one; it is the affective component which is present when there is laughter, or an actual physiological expression of enjoyment. The description therein is much like Freud's and the humor-release theorists— the experience is free from reason, coming when there is excess tension that somehow has to be worked off.

Different from the *ha ha* experience is Karl Buhler's *a ha!* experience. This is when an individual gains a sudden insight or illumination—the *I've got-it* sensation.

Koestler explains this as an intellectual or logical experience wherein, after searching for a missing link, one finds it, sighs with relief, but only after experiencing the high of the *a ha!* The tension released through this experience is very different from Koestler's *ha ha* release. As he puts it,

"When you look at a clever New Yorker cartoon, Homeric laughter yields to an amused and rarefied smile; the ample flow of adrenalin has been distilled into a grain of Attic salt."

Herein, Koestler remarks admirably, "the clown is brother to the sage."

Koestler's second domain is akin to the experience of creative discovery, and is different from the experience of affective humor.

The "ah" domain is Koestler's third category, and this seems to parallel the approach of the humanistic psychologist, an event akin to Maslow's "peak experience." Koestler sees this reaction as opposite to that exploded in laughter. He equates the laughing, *ha ha* reaction to the adrenalin-pounding, hunger-rage, fear category, indicating its primal quality. But the *ah* reaction is integrative and participatory. Koestler feels that in this reaction, the self relates itself to the universal.

This third realm of activity, for Koestler, is typified by "self-transcending emotions," which are experienced in union, not in antagonism with others. So we enter the arena of those who know that ecstasy is not a product of relief alone.

Many of us feel that when the boundaries of self are extended or transcended, there is growth and the knowledge that, although the experience may seem to be internal and totally personal, one has "travelled" a great distance. These realizations illustrate a positive image of man and the belief that men and women, in discovering a new meaning out of old forms, may truly *put* meaning into their lives. Through such actions, we confirm that the human condition carries within it joy as well as sorrow. We find these kinds of highs again and again in our interviews.

Our specific hope at this point is that you will be able to understand and recognize these components of the creative process as well as appreciate the many kinds of pleasure evoked through creativity as Norman Lear shares his life with you. It is our further hope that through the medium of his words, you will be led to understand how Norman's creative genius allows him to *add time to his own life.*

Interview

Fry: Mr. Lear, perhaps you could tell us the story of how your career got started. How did you break into this very special, very demanding, very competitive field?

Lear: I was always funny, they tell me, when I was a kid. I started off *being* funny physically, not writing or wanting to write, but being funny. I think I was in pain, I think most of it comes out of pain. I came from a family who yelled a great deal. They lived at the top of their lungs always. The only defense against that was to laugh at it, find what was funny in it. Like somebody begging somebody for something, for anything. Let that somebody crawl on their knees across a room, follow somebody around on their knees—that can be funny—and terrible. I had lots of those kinds of sights during my youth to frighten me, but also to make me laugh and see what was funny.

I did a scene in, "Divorce American Style" where a little boy listening to his mother and father fight was scoring them, making points. Well, that was myself, I did that. I used to sit in the kitchen in full view of them, and have a pad and pencil and I would be scoring them. What could I do? They paid no attention to me, they didn't know what on earth I was doing, I don't even remember what I said, if anything. Nobody paid any attention whatever to my presence. I was largely an observer, and I wouldn't get involved, except to carry those valises to the subway station when mother left the one time. She walked out. She got to a fever pitch and finally took two bags, and I walked her to the subway station because she was going to leave. And then we walked back, she never really left. My mind is cluttered with incidents like that. "All in the Family" reflects some of them. I remember my mother chasing my grandfather across the floor on her knees—with her hands like this, "I beg of you, I beg of you," she was saying, asking him to stop saying something he was saying. Or my father was in the heat of a big argument. I could either go to pieces or find something humorous in this. And I found something funny in it, because I also knew that everything was going to be—if that was 5 o'clock, I knew by 7:30 everything would be the way it was at 4 again so—

F: It was a three generation household?

L: Well, no, except at holidays. Some of the loudest arguments would take place at holidays and funerals —those were "fun" get togethers. It would be over Christmas, or they might be there for a whole week. On Passover, they'd be there for a whole week.

F: In your early life, was there anybody you knew personally who was very jolly, or had a good sense of humor, or who was a humor model or inspiration for you?

L: In retrospect, in recent years, I have realized what a marvelous sense of humor my grandmother possessed. My mother's mother. I lived with her for a couple of years when I was ten or eleven, something like that, ten to twelve. In her later years, she became an invalid in an old people's home. But the last thing to go is that glint of humor. On one visit, as I left her I said, "Bye bye, I'll see you. I'll see you again soon." And she said, "I'll be here. If I'm here, I'll be here." It was the reading, and intimation. She was in this condition and yet said these most incredible things. Nobody else on either side of the family had a sense of humor like that.

F: And your grandmother—did she make any observations of the family turmoil? Did she lead you in any fashion to handle this in a humorous way?

L: She was the subtlest, loveliest influence on my life, and I realize it more in the last ten years, the feeling I had when I used to visit her when she was in the home, after my grandfather died. She started to grow on me because I saw her and this lady was blind and totally enfeebled —this incredible sense of humor that was with her to the end, and that took me back over the years where I realized it was always there, always there, and I just hadn't appreciated it as much.

About my father's family. An uncle gave me instructions at the age of 7, I guess it was, on how to properly pee as a little boy. He did this at five in the morning, when I had gotten up. It was in the Depression, my father's parents had a cottage in Woodmark, Connecticut. All of the sons and daughters used to come out there with their children so that there'd be six kids sleeping in one room and two couples in another room, and two couples in another, my grandparents in another room in this little cottage. And I don't know how we all got into that cottage. But early one morning—these little cottages are made of—the wood is paper thin, and I was in the bathroom early one morning, a little boy, and suddenly the door burst open, slammed open, banged against the wall, and my uncle Ed was standing there—he screamed at the top of his voice. "I'm going to show you something you'll never forget the longest day you live. When you go into the bottom of the bowl" and he proceeded to show me, "this is the noise you will hear, but you see the empty porcelain on the side, listen—you hear that, no noise," and he said "don't you forget that, the longest day you live" and he slammed out of the room and in about five minutes the whole house was up and it wasn't six o'clock yet. That was one of the first episodes I wrote up professionally—never sold it. But got it to Joe Lewis as a routine. And I remember how he used to explain what it was about. It was about this universal truth that unites mankind—all mankind, black, yellow, red and white, every man understands that water sprayed on water makes a sound all through the air, but water sprayed on porcelain falls silent to the ears. That's a simple truth.

Allen: Did you have relationships based on humor with anybody you grew up with, outside of the family?

L: Well, I had friends when a young teenager. We put on shows at a social club we belonged to. One kid thought he wanted to be in show business, he wanted to be a comedian and did indeed become a comedian. We knew each other about two years, and in the little period that I knew him we kidded about some day putting an act together, but I was never serious about being a performer. I never really wanted to be a performer. The few plays I did in college scared the hell out of me. I couldn't ever wish to do that as a career.

As a response to "All in the Family," I got a letter recently from a family who lived next door to us in the apartment we moved into when we went to New York from New Haven. This family was living in the apartment next door to us and the man is now some 80 years old, and in the last two months I've heard from that whole family as the result of "All in the Family"—so I was reminded of a great many things. One of them concerned a daughter my age, reminded me of shows that we used to put on in the backyard in Lincoln Place. I'd forgotten, but I remember so clearly now. I would write whole plays and do a performance with six acts of vaudeville or something, have all the kids in it. We used to do it for pennies instead of selling lemonade. They reminded me of "King Lear and the Harmonica Maniacs." We were four kids who taught each other how to play the harmonica, and we used to rehearse on the roof. The show was on the ground and the rehearsal on the roof. We went to an amateur night in some theatre some place in Flushing—it was quite a distance from home, and we took second prize. I was about 14 years old then. We lived in New York two years. Then we moved to Connecticut, to Hartford.

F: Did you put on shows in Hartford?

L: Well, I guess—that was the time I started to write—I started to write a column for my high school newspaper. Weaver High School. It was an interview column. On a couple of occasions when entertainers came to town—I loved the Ritz Brothers at that age—I remember a picture I have which was printed in the Lookout, which was the newspaper. I still have a copy of "Leering Lear and the Rolicking Ritz" which was my own caption—and I'm standing between the Ritz Brothers leering—I did an interview with them. I used to go to the State Theatre in Hartford. It was the biggest theatre in New England. Had more people on the ground floor, or something. It was huge, and it was the home in that area of the great band shows, Goodman and Artie Shaw, and those great, great band shows. I suffered through a dozen lessons, or a couple of dozen trumpet lessons. I suffered through these lessons that I hated—I hated the teacher, and I hated the bloody trumpet lessons, but I suffered with them so that my family would let me go every Saturday to the State Theatre where the band was incidental to the rest of the show, and I would sit there all day and watch eight or ten shows. I was ostensibly, as far as my family was concerned, sent there to study the trumpet player.

F: Do you remember any of the shows you put on in New York?

L: Oh, no.

A: Did you have any audience for the kind of thing you were doing then?

L: I had an audience, among my peers, and their parents.

F: Your grandmother?

L: My grandmother, no, because she didn't read English, and she wouldn't know a good deal about what was happening with me.

A: You had by then become a funny guy. Did your parents respond to that?

L: Yes. In my early teens I was a kind of "lampshade" kid, I guess. I mean putting lampshades on one's head, getting dressed in girl's clothing at parties—those things that kids do.

F: This was at home that you did the practical jokes, kidding around?

L: Yes. It was very funny and very "on" and I'm sure very trying.

F: You don't have any of the scripts of these shows tucked away in a trunk somewhere? Did you write out scripts for the various shows?

L: I doubt it. I see the mothers sitting there in the yard, on concrete. I can see the women sitting there and I can see the orange crates or whatever we had to stand on—that's the stage, but I don't remember what we did. Then I remember poems I did about the daughter of the family that wrote to me recently and her sister. In that same period I wrote—do you want to hear one of my priceless poems?

F: Yes.

L: It's all in the reading. I wrote this at that same time.

City Lights

As you walk up Times Square you will notice here and there,
In fact, you'll notice everywhere, City Lights,
And as you stroll down Broadway—
You hear the people say, City Lights.
Some advertising Wrigley, others mentioning Squibbs,
Still others announcing a new kind of baby's cotton bibs,
To a foreigner it's marvelous, while to us it gets monotonous.
We want to live where we won't have to hustle,
Yet they yearn for your hustle and bustle.
Rich man, poor, beggerman and thief,
Men like Roosevelt and Walter O'Keefe,
They enjoy walking around on valuable ground,
That's City Lights.
      Norman Lear, age 11, Second Prize,
      Nick Kenny Contest, New York Daily Mirror

That's when my folks sat up, for 10 minutes. They commissioned me to write a poem for their next anniversary. The poem was in the first show of "All in the Family"—I wrote it for my father, "All the years I have been with you, I have shed many a tear"—remember that? He had a gift for my mother and he wanted a little expression and I wrote the poem. He liked the poem so much that he never told my mother I wrote it, and had it framed. It hung for all the years I lived at home in the ante room in our house, when we moved to Hartford. My mother has it, I don't think she knows to this day that was dad's poem that was in the TV show.

My first real contact with show business started when I was in Italy, the war had ended. I always wanted to be in publicity in show business—that was the extent of what I knew I wanted to do—I had an uncle who during the Depression was the only relative who would flip a half a buck to me. Either he could afford it, or couldn't afford it, but he had some flair, and he flipped it.

So I wanted to be in publicity. When the war ended and I knew I was going to be coming back, I went to a printer in Fugie, Italy. I remember standing over his shoulder a whole afternoon, showing him which piece of type to pick up, which I had trouble reading backwards, and he printed this announcement of my impending discharge and availability to publicity houses in New York, Chicago and Los Angeles. And from that silly thing I had two offers—I had an offer from George Evans, who was the guy who made Frank Sinatra, and I had an offer from George Ross, who had a well known publicity house in New York. When I got back to the States I saw my uncle, and he said to go with Dorothy and George Ross, "that's a better place to work" for whatever reasons I don't know. So I went to work there, and that was the first association. I was writing jokes and making up extravagant pieces of news for Dorothy Kilgallen and Walter Winchell and Leonard Lyon, and all the people whose columns are really written by these young kids who eventually become writers. Ernest Lehman started that way, and Paul Gallico started that way, and I don't know how many—hundreds of guys all started that way. Most of the guys out here, many of them my age did.

A: Then what?

L: Then I was making $40 and asked for $45 and was fired. And I couldn't afford to live in New York. I tried to get a job in other places in publicity but couldn't and I had a wife who was about to have a new baby, our first baby, so we went back to Hartford, where it was much cheaper living. I had a design patent on an ashtray that clipped to a coffee saucer, which I called the "demi-tray," and got into manufacturing. I went to New York and found a distributor who said they were just beautiful, "could you get them silver-plated?" It was a great Christmas season in 1946. Carol Stupell was selling demi-trays, that was a leading gift shop in New York, still is, Madison Avenue. She carried them in Sterling silver, the stupid little demi-tray. And then we took the money we made and we invested it in tools and dies for other products. We were going to have a big gift line, and we made a classic mistake—we didn't have any more ideas. It was some kind of a fluke that I had the demi-tray idea. It wasn't my kind of thinking at all. I don't know how it happened, so what we had to do was borrow ideas. So we knocked off other products. But I didn't know that when you knock off other products, you have to knock them down—you see something you like in Sterling silver and you decide to make it in silver plate, or you see something in silver plate and you decide to make it in copper. What was $4 you can sell for $2. We saw something in copper and made it in silver plate. We went right on our asses and Hartford didn't look good any more, and publicity and theatre did again. But not in New York, so I piled my wife and daughter in the car and came to California.

F: What did you do here?

L: I sold baby pictures. I sold baby pictures—you know, one of these jobs you join a crew of guys and they drive you out to what is called 'territory' and you're left off in your territory and you walk down the street and make appointments for a photographer to come and take pictures, offering one big photo for nothing, or something.

Oh, I remember another job I had in that period. I used to walk around—I thought it was so funny—I walked around from door to door with a large lamp—and that's what the company called it, "a large lamp"—or a ship clock, as a gift. "Lady, this is a gift." "I don't believe you." "It's a gift, it's yours." "Look, I don't want to look at it." You'd turn around and then over your shoulder you'd say, "I'll be back a little later." Some days I'd go with the ship clock and say, "Which would you like, the large lamp or a ship clock?" And then sell nine rooms of furniture later.

So with the baby pictures I would make the appointment and then come back a few days later with the proofs, and the promise, of course, probably that the ladies would get a big picture for nothing, she had to buy $1.95 worth, or something like that. And then you tried to get a $50 sale—people with babies and pictures, anything is possible. I was terrible at it.

A: How did you make the first show biz contact out here?

L: I met a guy when I was doing this thing. His name was Ed Simmons. He wanted to write publicity and he wanted to be a comedy writer. We got along well going out on the territory, occasionally he would be dropped on one street with his ship clock and I'd be on my street with my large lamp, and we'd have a four hour lunch and think the ship clock and large lamp were very funny. We decided to have our wives meet, and they met. The four of us were friendly. One evening after we had been out in the territory together, and the girls went to a movie, he had an idea for a parody. We wrote the parody in about a half hour—a parody on The Shiek of Araby. It was a dirty parody and he said it would be great for a girl named Virginia May. She played at Larry Potter's, on Ventura Boulevard—it used to be way out—and I mean way out West, when the town was smaller. When the girls came home from the movie, we went over to Virginia May's and got $25 for it, the song and words. She loved it. That was $25 we had made in half an hour, it was just absolutely —we couldn't believe it. So we took an office, over a little delicatessen on Beverly Boulevard, and the smell from the corned beef was unbelievable. We paid $5 a month, and next to us were Goldberg and McCormack, songwriters. Goldberg and McCormack had the whole front of the building painted with "Goldberg and McCormack" and had a staff and music on the sign. They had slogans which I can't remember, and they never sold a thing, to my knowledge. We had that office to write at night because the days and weekends we were selling baby pictures, and we sold maybe a dozen pieces of material like that for $50. We were paid $1 a week sometimes. Guys weren't making much money then. There was an ex-fighter, former heavy-weight champion, Lou Nova. Lou was going to have an act once. He was going to be a comic, and a fellow by the name of Thad Swift was going to be a straight man, and they had a pig. Thad Swift and his pig. We were hired, and we wrote an act for Thad Swift, Lou Nova and a pig. We went out to Santa Monica on a Saturday afternoon—some show they were going to do, and there were like eleven people in the audience in this terrible theatre, and the whole thing was such a terrible bomb. We never wanted to get paid, it was all so frightful, and what we wrote was terrible—we hated it. That's the kind of thing that was going on then.

I had a boyhood friend back East by the name of Merle Robinson. I always loved that name so much I had used it whenever I was stopped in the Army by the Military Police. I had used it for all kinds of other things. If I didn't want a girl to know my name, I said I was Merle Robinson. So one day I called William Morris, who represented Danny Thomas. Because I didn't know how I'd reach a star such as Danny Thomas from that little office above the delicatessen, I said, "This is Merle Robinson and I am out here for the New York Times." That I had a couple of show business stories and was on my way back to New York. There was some information I needed for a piece I was writing on Danny Thomas. And I had to reach him now. The urgency in my voice and the fact I was from the New York Times, this girl gave me a number and I called the number and Danny Thomas answered the phone. I said "I have a fantastic piece of material for you—you don't know me, but I have a fantastic piece of material for you." "How did you get my number?" And I don't remember what I said. But he was with his accompanist, Walter Prock, and they were trying to figure out what they were going to do two nights later at a Friar's Frolic at Ciro's. The show business community knew everything he had done, and he wished he had something new. This was going on as I called him, and he said, "I have never done this before, but how fast can you be here?" And we hadn't written a thing, it wasn't written, it was just a great idea. And I said, whatever the excuse was, I don't know, "It will take a couple of hours." He said, "OK, we're working, come with the idea." We sat down, wrote it. He had given us his address, we went to his house. He read it aloud, loved the part, and fell down. And he did it and he probably still does it now and then. An agent who was at that Friar's Frolic called the next morning and said, "Have you ever written television, you guys?" I said, "Yes," and he said, "Can I see some sketches?" And I said, "Sure," and he was going to leave town the next day. I went to my landlord and got a television script from him that he had around the house—I didn't even know how those things were put on paper. In those days there was audio on one side and video on the other side. Ed and I sat down and wrote three sketches, audio-video. The agent took them back to New York with him the next day, and like four days later we were back in New York writing the Jack Haley Ford Star Revue, an hour show a week and that was the beginning.

A: What about yourself in the creative act—at the moment of creativity? Can you give us a picture of before you get to the machine, while you are there—any kind of a picture of the sequence of things you go through?

L: I'll tell you some things I've never before said aloud. It has occurred to me, and I would never know how to write it down myself. The first feelings I have when I'm ready to write are I'd like to get laid, or masturbate. I want—it's physical, I want to make love, I want to—it's that, and if I'm not careful I'll do the sex and then not be there to do the writing. The last thing that happens in the writing is an extended orgasm which could be for a week, a month or whatever, when everything is going so well that it's just one large—orgasm is the only word with which to describe it. Everything is gushing, everything is just gushing. When it's going well, the difficult problems are behind you, or maybe there are even a few out there still, that you know you're going to beat, you just know you are going to go around those trees or climb that mountain or whatever those obstacles are, you just know, and you can't wait to find out how you are going to do it, and so it and the sex drive—the creative and sex drive are very related.

A: Moravia wrote a book saying something like you're saying now. The lead character goes off to write a novel in Italy. He is just newly married to a woman, and he literally has to shut her away from him because he can't do both at the same time—like a reserve of energy that is there, it is either spent on the writing for him or on this woman he loves, but he definitely makes an analogy between the two things. What about the bad times, when it's not gushing? Tell us what you go through at those times.

L: I go through—before I get to this nicer time, I go through this—sometimes it can be long, sometimes longer—never short—period which I identify as "shit in the head"—that's the only way I have ever described it to myself. I just have a kind of an aching band about three inches wide, around the head. It isn't tightened into a headache. It is something that is just aaaah, like a sound. And I am afraid nothing is going to come through this morass, nothing is going to escape or come through, and I can't motivate myself to do anything, let alone, least of all, write. There is a period like that usually before each writing situation. Say I'm only three weeks from rehearsal. Three weeks from today I'll be in rehearsal, and I spend too much of my time wondering which thing to do. There are so many things I have to get ready. Which ones to get to now, which later on—months from now, or never, or tonight? Your mind is wrestling with the things you are going to do this week. I don't always recognize it—I dig at myself because I am not actually writing every second that I think I should.

Let me tell you the story about my famous writer friend. I was talking to him one day. He's a very prolific writer. And I told him I had just signed for motion pictures that I had written, I had produced and I had directed, and I had worked very hard on. I was home three days after shooting was completed after a really giant job. Anybody would have been happy to give himself a week's rest. I find myself standing in my living room, marrying my daughter off to a young man I adore, and feeling in the course of this ceremony a strange sense of guilt. And I suddenly realized, "I'm not working," and I was just flooded with this—you know, the immensity—the incredible thing—I'm standing a foot from—and the rabbi is incanting and I'm feeling "why am I not writing?" So I told this to my friend who said to me that it had happened to him only a few days before. "Norman, I was standing at my mother's grave and they were lowering the casket" and he didn't have to say any more. Even at a funeral he was thinking about it—and I think that's a kind of thing about writers.

F: How do you break the writer's blocks? Special techniques?

L: In recent years I have learned to force myself to make notes, little mechanical things that I'll do. To make notes I use a tape recorder. I get started with a tape recorder, usually. *Start something,* in the last ten years that's what I've learned to do. It will get me into a fair start, without pages that call my attention to them, and without sentences that are there for me to rewrite.

A: Just you talking out loud into it?

L: No, I do script in it, and talk to myself at the same time.

F: Where do you start—beginning, at the middle, or the end of the script?

L: Well, the actual script I always start at the beginning, and if I don't really know the beginning, I will talk about the beginning endlessly. I let myself get into the second part.

A: You have a better feeling about beginning at the beginning?

L: Yes.

F: That's even before you get the idea?

L: No—not before I get the idea.

F: The idea comes first, then.

L: An outline of what it's going to be comes first, even if that outline is in my head. I have to know before I can begin that, a beginning and an ending.

F: You talk—when you're actually working on the script. You get yourself on a tape recorder. You mentioned some other things—what other things? You mentioned some mechanical things.

L: By mechanical I mean something like writing the first idea that comes into my head—whatever that idea is, even if it has nothing in the world to do with the story. "To find a hairpin"—whatever it is.

A: You are giving yourself little pieces of stimulation —to turn yourself on?

L: Well no, somebody once said to me, "Ideas, if you don't let them out, are like somebody yelling fire and everybody rushing to a door." If everybody rushes to the door, the door doesn't get open and nothing gets out, but if you open the door and let them out one at a time, they might all get out, and so I always try to keep that in mind. If I cannot get to what it is that I want to say, let the other things out first. If I am thinking "shit," I write "shit."

F: Do you have any other analogies that you work with in your mind, other than the fire and the door?

L: For that particular thing, no.

F: Now, say we have gotten beyond this block then, and you are actually composing. What do you find yourself usually thinking about—do you think about sex or do you think about the content of the material—what is your mind taken up with?

L: It depends. If the muse is going well, and ideas are flowing freely, then I am into what I am doing. If not, I am thinking about sex, or a great many other things in my field. When I'm writing a screenplay, I have the most wonderful ideas for plays, novels, short stories—wonderful ideas, getting presidents elected, and I love to communicate with Congress at that time.

A: Let's say you are in a situation where you are writing. You are at the typewriter, and you're writing, and you are in some sort of situation in the middle of a scene. You really feel you are in that scene. Do you picture—are you visualizing—what does the inside of your head look like?

L: Right in that scene. I am seeing and hearing everything.

A: How does your body feel?

L: It depends on what my eating habits have been for the weeks preceding. I feel best when I'm hungry, when I'm lacking a little. I feel terrible when I've over-eaten.

A: Can you give us any kind of a picture of what "terrible" is, or what "good" is?

L: It depends on how it is going, really, as to what my attitude is. I can feel warm, I can feel like my posture's bad, my breath is bad, my feet smell, my beard is ugly, I can feel absolutely lousy and everything wrong with me if it's going poorly. If it's going very well, all of those things can indeed be true but I'd not be aware of any of them.

F: You get carried away by your own jokes which you are creating?

L: I get carried away completely. If I write something really funny it will—you know, I can add time to my own life.

F: What's the most important thing to do at that point—to laugh, to share with somebody else, write it down, or—

L: To tell somebody, which isn't necessarily what should be done, but it's my compulsion, what I have to do. Many times I have told it before it was completed—it was completed for me, but it was not completed for telling, for transmitting, and I've hurt myself by bouncing it against somebody who could give me no response. I haven't had a collaborator in a great many years. I've written alone for so long now that this kind of thing has happened to me—writing into a thing and knowing it was funny, and then finding more and more and then just becoming overjoyed with it. That happens sometimes too with something you know you will never be able to use, just some insight or something. God, how you wish you could share this, or some little something you can't even tell anybody.

A: With you as Norman, at home or wherever you are, I'm wondering if you're funny. Are you funny at the same time as you're being spontaneous, or do you have that kind of feeling that you are seeing yourself?

L: Yes. That is a problem of mine. It's true, but I'm not proud of it. I do see myself—I always see myself, I'm much too aware of myself all the time. The only exception to that is in that period which I described as an extended orgasm thing, when I can just lose myself completely. And the best things I do come out of that, but otherwise I'm very conscious of myself.

A: Have you seen yourself as a writer using humor where it might be truly painful for another person or maybe inappropriate to the scene you are really in?

L: No, I can't remember when I made that mistake. Maybe I've done it unconsciously. I can't really remember.

There's a whole—in this humor world—there's a whole breakdown of areas where it's inappropriate to use humor—such and such a time. It's an unwritten rule, a gentleman's agreement that you don't—at certain times.

F: Do you have any rules about creating humor?

L: No. I don't think there can be any rules. There are people I know who write books on how to write humor. I don't know how you can list rules to write humor, writing anything. I visited with a man who conducted writing classes. I spent a few sessions with him, and I learned that anybody born with instincts can get in trouble with those rules, any set of rules. And I guess anybody who really wants to write very much, and doesn't have the instinct, maybe can use the rules.

A: For you though, when it really works, it's an instinctive kind of thing?

L: Instinctive. And when you say, "why?" because my belly tells me. I have rewritten one little thing repeatedly over a period of weeks, just a line, no longer—I don't mean to the exclusion of everything else, but I could come back to things like that time and time again until my head and my belly were satisfied.

A: You have a pretty clear message, being sent to you if it doesn't work for you?

L: Right, and if it does, I know it's right. And if it doesn't. But it's there somewhere, the message is clear. I can't really think about it too hard. It would destroy what's necessary in entertainment to think too much about what I'm writing. I've learned, by looking backwards, that I've always said something, in everything I've ever done. Every scene I've ever worked on had something for me. I learned this looking backward on it, but I can't do it looking forward. I can't think about what am I going to do or say next because I lose the sense of spontaneity and fun. I'm content that I'm going to present reasonably new ideas with reasonable affection and respect, and they'll hit targets, but I can't think a lot about that or I'll destroy the whole kick I'm on. I love looking back, I like to look at last night's show—"Gee, I had something there, that was nice." And I can see why people are saying this and that. People surprise me all the time by seeing other things I never thought about.

Summary

Norman Lear reigns over a not-too-small "monarchy" in the television industry. We interviewed him just prior to the blossoming of his success—just after his first Emmys were taken home.

   In studying his life, we see that humor has, from his earliest years, played a vital part in his life—a part which initially had little to do with mechanics or with deadlines.

And Norman claims that the creation of humor still is far from an habitual routine or a mechanical endeavor.

Although one or two of our other writers seemingly live detached from the humor they create, Norman clearly demonstrates that humor is an integral part of his life-style and philosophy of life. Indeed one of his first interview lines was, "What brings *you* here today, Doctor?" Vestiges of his early slapstick routines often manifest themselves spontaneously.

In his first descriptions of his life as a boy, watching his mother in a rather pitiful battle for existence, waiting for ships to come in, and seeing sights that could have frightened him, early on Norman discovered that absurdity fused with what frightened to make him "laugh and learn to see what was funny."

At that stage Norman clearly used humor as a defense—making up a series of routines that helped him cope with long periods of tension and which prevented him from exploding at those around him. Freud could have proved his theory with Norman! When his mother had stopped waiting for ships to come in or for people to "save the show," and demonstrated her strain and worry on a daily basis, Norman slapsticked around the place, turned his eyelids inside out (as he did for us, by the way, becoming a child again, playing with and for us). Norman became a master of the *ha ha* experience, distracting others from antipathy, turning them on, and making himself feel better—even relieved in the process.

The eyelid routine and the physical activity of slapstick became refined when Norman became the observer, scoring his parents on their wins and losses at the kitchen table. Again, however, he is on the defense, again distracting himself and keeping his ear open for the choice line, the funny moment in the midst of what must have been a painful and chaotic family life for a young boy.

Later, as Norman told us, he would directly lift such moments from out of the past into situations made famous in his movie and television scripts. In other words, he would relive and rediscover some of the same tragicomic moments that were never completely repressed in his youthful mind and memory.

Learning theorists or behaviorists might say that this habit of converting tragedy into comedy from early days on would form the entire basis for a personality—that Norman's indentity would come from having to defend in this way. But humanistic psychologists would view this coping and establishing a humorous identity as something postitive—indicative of the attempt of a young boy to use his strengths, his potential to attain security in the midst of chaos, rather than merely to escape the scene.

During the Walter Winchell years, Norman's style stayed that of the "gagman"—the style that earned him a sure audience among both family and peers when he was in high school. As were several of our writers, Norman was a gag ghostwriter for Winchell, but before he was to get his first big break in show business, a long period of "funny little businesses" came first.

A good example of this is the Merle Robinson segment in his interview. The combination of the "old buddy Merle" and the many situations in which Norman utilized that name is, of course, an excellent example of on-the-spot invention. We expect that Norman was giving us the true story, but also, suspect that as he saw us obviously tickled at the details, he might have elaborated a bit on them. This is our concept of building upon the creation of the *ha ha* experience—on the spot. This is the concept of a rehearsal hall, one might say, for the act of putting it all down on paper—as a professional creator.

We feel the Merle Robinson story is both a good example of semi-audacious and self-assertive behavior (Norman's ability to strike out and get what he wants), and the kind of story that turns him on, no matter how many times he tells the story. This story typifies his approach both to his work and to living his life. When we interviewed his wife, Frances, she was extremely helpful in reinforcing our impression that, to live in the Lear family, you *have* to be able to laugh at others and at yourself. Often, heavy moments are broken by that slight twist which makes the tragic absurd. Is this pattern hurtful to others? Norman hopes not. He certainly doesn't mean it to be. But, as in his childhood, he is ever alert to the humor in domestic life, and his family ambiance involves a group of individuals who, like Norman, parlay the jokes, roll with the punches, and better each other's lines.

Norman *is* aware that he still waits for some manner of applause. "Being on" is not unusual, and he feels that if he is too "sensitive to audience," it could ruin his native spontaneity. Yet, we join him in agreeing that this type of group-consciousness can also make his writing and his choice of materials successful.

He is not possessive of his materials. When "All in the Family" hit the air, he held weekly sessions pre-show wherein he asked audience members to help him develop scenes, make choices as to which behavior seemed most appropriate to certain characters, or which one of two or three lines was the funniest.

This is the analyst, the scientific creator, probing for the craftsmanlike approach; but, for Norman, humor is customarily a visceral reaction. If it is learned, it becomes "like an instinct." He waits for the "click," the *"a ha* experience."

Some of our most valuable material was provided by Norman in his detailed description of the creative process as it exists for him.

If you look carefully over his interview, you will find that, with no coaching from us as to the theory of stages and/or phases, Norman's description parallels that of Koestler and others, clearly crossing beyond the bounds of drive-reduction theorists.

In his initial stage, one of preparation or anticipation, he has clearly described the tension involved, and how he must hold onto the tension, even forcing it to increase, lest he spend the energy in other ways. The second stage, which he calls "shit in the head," wherein he is often isolated, confused, and "feeling mentally and physically terrible" clearly parallels the incubation period described by some of the theorists we have mentioned. This period finds him in a further building of tension, searching for a "hairpin," often existing in a blur. Interestingly enough, although Norman didn't attach any formal label to this period, his wife, Frances, did. She calls it his gestation period and shows a good understanding of what he described going through. Similar to creativity theorists, Frances does not see this period as wasteful. She understands that with the "commingling of images," one fragment may touch off other associations. We see this as the gradual integration of an *appreciative mass; creative synthesis.*

Frances describes Norman as being preoccupied and non-communicative during this stage. Her knowledge of his need to be alone is an exact echo of what he told us. This is the period in which he gets restless, stir-crazy, conjuring up thoughts of any way to escape rather than to write, like having sex or even communicating with his congressman.

And then Norman describes a transition into:

> ". . . a wonderful period, also physical which could last for a week or a month, when everything is going so well it's just, well, the only way to describe it is one extended orgasm . . . everything is gushing, everything is just gushing . . . the muse is with you . . ."

Looking back over that lovely section and the description that follows, of Norman's feeling of indomitability, of "climbing that mountain or whatever you call those obstacles," Norman has obviously given us his personal expression of the emergence from the pain and strain of the incubation period to the "extended orgasm" of illumination directly into the period of productivity.

We are interested in his feeling that this state of soaring elation and supreme well-being can last for the entire period of production to follow. And this is when he made the remark that so struck us, we chose it to open this section:

> "You know, I can get carried away completely . . .
> And I can add time to my own life."

We join Koestler and others of the humanistic bent. We cannot equate Norman's expression as being evidence of tension-release alone. Rather than the sudden and short-lived ecstasy found in sexual orgasm, he lasts it out, reaching for that "peak of pleasure" which holds for him, and for most creators, a very different kind of power. Albeit he utilizes the metaphor of sex, that metaphor which has become so typical of the twentieth century and of America; he has, perhaps despite himself, given incredible scope to this period of culmination. He demonstrates that the *ah* experience named by Koestler and the intense enjoyment experienced in the contemplation of what one has made for himself and for others is *real*. For Norman Lear, creativity ends in a prolonged period of expansiveness, accomplishment, that self-fulfillment which comes to this man only in the act of invention. As creator-inventor, he feels the full impact of personal power. *He recreates himself.*

And, if all of us aimed only to return to homeostasis, simply to escape from pressure and tension into the most basic sort of pleasure, *why*, just after "having finished a giant job," would Norman stand at the wedding of his daughter and feel again the void of not-writing coming over him? We suggest that this is because the experience of creativity and the emotional and intellectual challenge it poses for him *is* the process of growth and of life. For him, the product has significance in that it signifies his ability to make connections, to overcome obstacles, to tame himself and to untame himself until a problem is solved. But, as with Sisyphus, it is the struggle, the process of trying to get there that magnetizes and mesmerizes him and brings him to begin again, naked and humble, so that he can again feel himself pushing himself, pulling himself out of the void.

Jack Elinson

*The Relationship of Humor to
Aloneness and Togetherness*

JACK ELINSON was born in 1922 in New York City. He was drafted into the Army in 1943, served in World War II. He entered the professional writing field in 1945. His hobbies are "jogging and tennis and going to the movies until my eyes get bleary."

He included the following paragraph when sending in his requested photograph for the book. "I wish I had one of those studied pictures of myself sitting behind my typewriter, deep in thought, creating the world's greatest comedy material . . . but the best thing I could find was this snap of me staring blankly ahead, with nary a joke in my brain."

As a writer he has written for Ed Wynn, Jimmy Durante, Garry Moore, the Real McCoys, and the Andy Griffith show. As a writer-producer he has worked on the Danny Thomas Show, Gomer Pyle, the Doris Day Show, among others. He is currently co-executive producer and co-script advisor on "Good Times."

In this interview, Jack Elinson speaks about differences between creating alone and creating in association with another writer. "You really have to be able to get along (with your partner). It's even more crucial than a marriage because you spend more time with your partner than you do with your wife. You have to have a rapport and be able to feed each other without destroying each other.

"Both my partner and I have worked alone in the past. That's another ball game . . . I would say that writing alone is harder, but probably . . . it's more rewarding—the feeling that you've done it all yourself. There is nothing that can elate you more than that."

One view of human beings sees us as rather lumpy bags of a very complex collection of chemicals, controlled in our behavior by a quite large, but finite number of extremely simple rules. Another view sees things quite differently, suggesting a variety of states which are both numerous and vital, and which are mutually influenced. They are presented as being so sophisticated that their ultimate relationships to the chemicals in the dermal bag are too obscure to demonstrate simple causality.

Before going on to Jack Elinson's interview, a little background material on the human states of *aloneness* and *togetherness* is in order here. Not only are these two states germaine to a study of humor, but they are also highly significant to the way all of us choose to live our lives.

Some tantalizing comments on these issues were offered by Polaroid inventor Edwin H. Land in 1970 at a Washington D.C. Cosmos Club address. Essentially, Dr. Land spoke of two special states of human functioning—that of "singular-man" and "multiple-man." Singular-man is that state of separateness from the rest of humanity, responding to a "violent need for being just yourself. You wish people would just go away and leave you alone while you get something straight." Dr. Land stated that serving oneself is the first function in the singular-man state.

The state of multiple-man is characterized as feeling part of the human race and its various subdivisions —family, community, and national groupings. Dr. Land indicated that the components of an individual "are intermixed with the components of other individuals to form the biological unit, the multiple-man." The individual vanishes "to become part of the composite creature, a social group. Through this group entity, feelings, thoughts, hopes, and speculations travel from boundary to boundary, resonating and reflecting within its confines. When the great symphonies of multiple-man echo through us, our individual conditioning, background, and predispositions introduce only trivial variations on a main theme."

These two states are considered by Dr. Land to be themselves of high importance. But he emphasized that the relationship between them is, in his eyes, of even greater significance. "It is this interplay between all that is richly human (multiple-man) and this special, concentrated, uninterrupted mental effort (singular-man) that seems to me to be the source, not only of science, but also of everything that is worthwhile in life." And, "The ready transition between modes (these two states) is the deepest of human needs, for without it man is either animal or derelict . . ."

Others have expressed their views on these states. In his book *Power and Innocence,* Rollo May wrote, "The future lies with the person who can live as an individual within the solidarity of the human race." An ecologic pronouncement summarizes the matter, "Man is impelled to congregate with his fellows, as is the case for other species. However, unlike other social creatures, he needs occasional brief episodes of isolation from other humans so as to reaffirm his solitude, independence, and self-sufficiency."

Several considerations lead us to believe that multiple-man state is the primary state, with singular-man state having developed as a mutational embellishment during man's climb up the evolutionary tree. Dr. Land suggested this possibility. Adaptional considerations favor the cooperative action found in multiple-man, and this state may represent the foundation from which humanity's movement advanced beyond caves and catch-as-catch-can hunting. However, for many people, the solitary state is an environment more conducive to *creative* inspiration.

Psychologist Thomas Kraft emphasizes the power of singular-man state. "People need time alone to recharge themselves. Being with other people takes up energy . . . you have to renew yourself by being alone . . . It's particularly good for the creative person, who needs an incubation period for ideas."

Jack Elinson writes with a partner, but together they isolate themselves out at the beach when starting a writing assignment. This choice can be seen as an attempt for simultaneous singular- and multiple-man states, in that they are thus deliberately isolated from peers, but are also together with each other.

Most of the values of the multiple-man state are obvious. Man is basically a gregarious creature and derives a deep satisfaction from the presence of fellows. Additionally, most emotional gratifications experienced by man come through the agency of association with others. And it is certainly clear that cooperative effort in the multiple-man state has raised more pyramids, crossed more oceans, played more symphonies, mined more ore than ever has the isolated efforts of a solitary person. It is less clear, but not a complete surprise, that much learning takes place best when done with others.

Unfortunately, these multiple-man values can be destroyed, as Goethe warned, by multiple-man involvement with people who are time-devourers. Goethe further warned, "He who wishes to do something for the world, must see to it that the world does not get the better of him." The benefits of the multiple-man state can be recognized as being as fragile as those of the singular-man state, and are dependent upon the association being truly multiple-man, not singular-man posing as multiple man. Or as Jack Elinson expresses it, "You have to . . . be able to feed each other without destroying each other."

There are several reasons for sluggishness of transition from one state to the other. One is that facility with transition is not a skill taught either in school or at home. Until very recently, with the worldwide interest in learning meditation techniques, any proficiency developed by an individual for shifting from one state to the other was accidentally acquired and practiced only through intuiton. Consequently, the average person finds either one or the other of these two states to be awkwardly attained when deliberately sought. Or, only through arduous effort and considerable self-sacrifice, is proficiency finally acquired.

Further, many people conscientiously seek to avoid transition from one state to the other. Being alone opens the doors to expansion of associations and frees thinking from conventional avenues of progress from one concept to the next. It promotes a widened range of distant and imprecise metaphor and enhances the possibility of that sudden recognition of relationships not previously realized, which is called creativity. (Traditional creativity theory is described: "Creativity is the process by which original patterns are formed and expressed.") This enhancement of creativity and fantasy would seem to make the alone state quite desirable. But many people are very uncomfortable in such circumstances. They much prefer the community multiple-man state with its many social reinforcements of personal identity.

On the other hand, many find difficulty with the multiple-man state. They seek in aloneness a buffer from potentially overwhelming confusion and trauma experienced in interpersonal life.

For these reasons, many people miss the benefit of easy transition between these two states. This deprivation would be especially regrettable if there were not certain human experiences in which people could naturally and automatically undergo both states.

And this brings us to the consideration of humor. Humor is the most common experience among those which frequently ameliorate the widespread deprivation resulting from people being stuck too much to one side of the alone-together dichotomy. Incidentally, closely related to humor in this regard are psychotherapy, shared spiritual enlightenment, and certain educational experiences. Sexual ecstasy, play and grief, when shared with others, have similarities to these other four, but are not so potent in the purity of special characteristics which are so vividly apparent in humor.

So, humor ameliorates deprivation. But not through some substituting or pacifying agent. It is not a distractive Roman carnival to take the mind of the populace off its troubles. Humor ameliorates as the result of its special "miracle" characteristics. These characteristics combine to make humor a microcosm of transition between alone and together. Humor provides simultaneous involvement in these states.

Humor is generally—not invariably, but generally—shared with other persons. From this standpoint, it is a multiple-man experience. People are amused together; they laugh together. Their mirth is potentiated by the mirth of others with whom it is shared; their laughter is potentiated by the laughter of those laughing with them. The social nature of humor is most obvious in the comedy of cultures and other group entities. Here, humor is found to play a dynamic role in the very evolution of the group, offering powerful mechanisms whereby the group unfolds its destiny. The power of these roles can be so great that the significance of humor to the individual may be obscured completely when observed in its function as social mechanism.

But, within the context of its social nature, humor is *always* a very individual experience. Humor depends on stimulating mental associations, fantasies, and realizations within the individual. Mirth will not result without the presence of mental associations implicit to the comedy content, which are precipitated by the humor punchline into explicit realization. In the last analysis, this implicit content, upon which mirth depends, must be stimulated in the individual mind of *each* humor maker or participant. The truth of this axiom is illustrated by the absence of mirth when someone "doesn't get the joke," and by the speed with which mirth disappears if someone calls on you to "explain the joke." The implicit content—mental associations—reflects common symbols, shared values, cultural assumptions, and social expectations. But it is within the individual brain that associations exist, whether on the conscious level or the unconscious.

Any felt, thought, or conceived content, of course, is a singular-man experience, in the sense that the content exists in individual brains. However, humor goes one step further, fulfilling that prediction of potent purity making it, as mentioned, the foremost frequent experience combining *alone* and *together*. This potency lies in the fact that humor is always an enlightening experience, involving self-discovery. In humor, one discovers that he knows something of which he wasn't aware. The art of the punchline is to express a truth which each member of the humor-audience suddenly recognizes as an old acquaintance, a bit of wisdom each has long possessed but had forgotten or hadn't seen before in quite that light. A significant part of the mirth derives from this self-discovery. If comedy is presented in an unknown language, or the allusions or images or concepts are foreign to the audience—so that nothing can be discovered about oneself—mirth does not result. If the comedy is trite or obvious to the audience, nothing new develops in the audience's self understanding, and no mirth occurs.

This quality of expansion of self-understanding is also found in psychotherapy, in shared spiritual enlightenment and in educational experiences of certain types. And since these are also experienced in unity with others, they afford the opportunity for *simultaneous* singular-man and multiple-man states. But, in comparison with humor, they are relatively *rare* occasions; and for this statistical reason, have less of this particular importance to the human race than does humor. Sexual ecstasy, play and shared grief are very intense individual and communal experiences—more so than most others; they have less of that element of self-discovery which makes humor so powerful on the singular-man side of the dichotomy. And so their contribution is less than that of humor.

A regrettably large number of people tend to regard humor, comedy, and mirth as frivolous, superficial, dispensible elements of human existence. They tend to dismiss creators of comedy—such as these comedy writers—with gentle condescension; they would regard humor material as undeserving of any special attention or interest. On the other hand, there are few people who do not recongize the vital importance of a person's commerce with himself, and his commerce with fellow humans. Few people would disagree with Dr. Land's comments on the deeper meanings of the singular-man and multiple-man states and the decisive value of experiencing both states. That humor presents to us all a common, pleasureful, easily-handled opportunity to undergo both states simultaneously indicates another value of humor, and another way in which people like Jack Elinson make life so much more fulfilling for so many of his fellow humans.

Interview

Allen: How did a nice guy like you get into this business?
Elinson: Well, actually, I got into this business via my brother. He was a writer, one of the original "gag writers" in radio. You know, in the days when people never realized the stuff was written at all; they thought the comedian just made it up as he went along. Writers in those days never even got credit at the end of a show like they do today on television.
Fry: When was this?
E: Well, let me just work back. My brother took up writing as a hobby. He got into it by sending jokes to Walter Winchell, and little by little, they got into his

column. In those days, Winchell was *the* columnist. He was the hottest columnist around. Press agents would try like mad to get their client mentioned in his column. You got the slightest mention and you were in. As a hobby my brother loved writing jokes. He started sending in jokes based on topical items—topical jokes, the kind Bob Hope would do today. He didn't get paid for them, but he would get his name in the column very often. This was the 30s, and I was about twelve or thirteen when he started this.

F: How old was your brother?

E: He was 24 or 25. He worked as a clerk for Borden's Milk Company. That was his regular job. He started sending in jokes and eventually became Winchell's biggest contributor of jokes. In fact, Winchell compared him to Will Rogers. He was brilliant with his topical jokes, and he became pretty well-known through the column. A lot of people would say, "Izzy Elinson says this . . . or Izzy Elinson observed that." Most people thought over the years that it was a made-up name, that there really wasn't such a person.

But he became very hot in the column, and still he was working for Borden's Milk Company. There was a comedian named Walter O'Keefe, who had a radio show. He was the tops in radio comedy then and he was looking for writers. He said, "Better get this guy, he's great" and offered my brother a job to come on the staff. It was a big crisis in my family because he was making $25 a week with Borden's and O'Keefe offered him $25 a week to start. It was a toss-up. My mother panicked. She said, "You're going to leave such a steady job as the Borden Milk Company and go into . . . who knew this kind of business, this writing job stuff?" No one had ever heard of such a thing. People in those days thought in terms of making a living, and kids grew up like that, too. So different from today. Most of us grew up pretty poor, in New York, in the tenements, we grew up with the fear of starving. We saw poverty all around, we saw struggling, and we feared it. My father was a house-painter and he worked all day long and dragged home at night and fell asleep. My mother was always panicky about money and trying to make sure we had it. And I was brought up in that atmosphere.

It was an automatic thing for a kid, the moment he could, to work and help support the family. That was routine, there was nothing else to consider. That's why money was such a big thing, a driving force. So for this new writing business, it was a whole new ball game, that started in radio in the 30s. The line was: "From this you can make a living?" Mom was petrified when he got the chance, and there was a lot of soul-searching that followed. Izzy finally decided to give up the job with Borden's to work full-time on the radio show. My mother was very unhappy. She sincerely thought he was making the mistake of his life. Later, his position on the show started improving and O'Keefe gave him a raise to $50, a whopping raise. Then she felt a little easier about it. The next raise was to $100. He eventually got up to $200, which, in those days, was equivalent to a thousand dollars today. After several years, my mother was finally convinced that maybe he'd made the right move. She still didn't really understand what it was all about, how a man could make a living from such a stupid thing but it was the Depression, and making $200 a week was being a millionaire, especially for us in the Bronx. So, brother pioneered the whole thing and made it easier for me. Because, when I was sixteen, still going to high school, I got the bug. I wanted to write jokes and I asked my brother what to do about it. He said, "Well, why don't you start the way I did, just send a few jokes in to Winchell."

F: Do you remember exactly when you got the bug, how it started?

E: No, I don't, and I guess if my brother hadn't been a writer, I wouldn't have been a writer. I think it's that simple. If someone in the family does something, like if your father owns a tailor shop, you become a tailor, it's like Elinson & Son. It's *there,* if your father is a doctor, the chances are pretty good, you might be a doctor.

F: How many were in your immediate family?

E: Five children, four boys and a girl. And let me say my whole family was very funny. I have many fond memories of absolutely roaring laughter around the dinner table. Everybody in the family had a great sense of humor, my father and mother included. I guess that's where it all came from. We lived all together, no one was married when I was a kid. My oldest brother was the first to get married and move away. Actually, he became a pharmacist, but, to this day, I think if he'd wanted to become a writer he could have, he's that funny.

A: Did you play off each other and do little family routines, set each other up, and the like?

E: Yes, just general clowning around. I remember doubling up with laughter most of the time. We had some pretty hysterical goings-on.

F: Can you remember any of the typical jokes?

E: No, it was just that everybody seemed funny. My sister is six years older than I am, and she says I was a riot when I was young, but I don't remember what I said or did, I know I just used to break her and her friends up. I wish I could remember exactly, but everybody had these funny lines. My father was the dry type, he had this sneaky humor, very dry, very quiet. But in his particular way, he could come up with some great lines. It seems like somewhere in our blood, there is a great deal of humor and it finally came out in my brother Izzy.

A: Were you boys pretty close?

E: Yes, my brothers and I were very close, especially after I decided to become a writer. Izzy was my motivating force, as I said. One day, he called up Winchell and said, "I've got a kid brother who wants to write jokes. Will you at least read them?" I started sending them in, and I got my first joke in Winchell's column when I was sixteen and still in high school. That was the biggest moment in my life. I was walking so cocky like I wanted to quit school and immediately go into joke-writing as a career.

F: Do you remember that joke?

E: Yes. A famous married Hollywood show biz couple had a violent argument and shot each other to death. Their last words were, "But we're still very good friends." You want to know something? This is still a very good joke that could be used today. And don't think I won't!

A: He was honest about his reactions?

E: Yes, and very tough to get into, he actually rejected more than he accepted. But, I sent him a bunch every day and was thrilled when I got some in. Still—I wasn't making any money out of it. Although my mother was conditioned now to having a joke-writer in the family, she really wanted me to become . . . you see, my oldest brother was a druggist, and she wanted to have me study pharmacology. She had visions of two brothers in a pharmacy together. But by then, I really had a bug about writing. I went to City College for a while; but the writing-bug was so deep in me. I felt I couldn't learn how to write; you can't learn how to write comedy in college. Oh, you can learn certain fine points and technical things, but I don't think there's a course in the world that can teach a guy how to be funny. I wish there were, but there isn't. You either have it, or you don't, to use the old cliché.

So I quit school, because I felt it was a waste of time. Now, I'm sorry, of course. I see my own son going through the same thing today. "What the heck am I going to college for? What good is it going to do me?" He's a musician.

Walter O'Keefe gave me a break, allowed me to make a few dollars when I was nineteen. He knew me through my brother and he had a radio show. His show was a kind of quiz show, called "Double or Nothing." They'd bring on contestants, and I would write the little patter, the little joke into the biographies of these contestants. If the man were a dentist, I'd write fourteen dentist jokes, give them to O'Keefe, and he'd pick whatever he wanted to use. They were all supposed to be considered *ad lib* by the audience. That was my little living. It wasn't very much, and it was cut short by the war.

F: How long did you work at that?

E: Oh, about a year or so, until I was drafted at twenty. The war was on. I entered the Army for three years. Only one time in the Army did I get to do any writing. It was really the funniest thing. I was stationed in Italy most of the time, in the front lines. One day a company clerk came up to me and said, "There's a phone call for you." It was just crazy, right there in the middle of Italy, and the war, and the first thing that hit me was—"Oh, my God, something has happened at home, and they're trying to reach me." I got on the phone and it was a writer who used to work with my brother when he was with Eddie Cantor. By then, he'd gone on to a lot of big shows. This guy was in the Army and he wanted to know if I could write a sketch, out of the blue. I figured this was a good way to spend the rest period I was on just then and also get me back into writing. This director, Ted Post, is now a big director in Hollywood, did Peyton Place on television, several movies. Anyway, I wrote a sketch, in long-hand, because there weren't any typewriters available. I based it on the Bill Mauldin characters, Willie and Joe—those old, dirty infantrymen. It was a funny sketch. The premise was that Willie and Joe go to a rest-camp. In those days they occasionally sent the front line soldiers back to a rest-camp for a little relaxation. These two dirty GIs in the sketch come into the rear echelon where the other soldiers are clean and kind of safe. I was told this revue was going to be shown to front line men, mostly, *not* the rear, so I figured—what is going to make a front line soldier laugh and love it? Naturally there was a bitterness between these two groups. The infantrymen hated the artillery being fifteen miles behind and safe all the time. The artillery men hated the quartermaster, and so on, it was a chain thing. And the guys who were most bitter were those right up front. So I sent the sketch in. A few months later, I happened to be in a rest period in Florence, Italy, and I saw ads on the wall that the show was playing. I dropped into the theater and there they were, rehearsing the sketch, and I met Ted Post. He was really excited to meet me, as though I were a kind of mystery name, or something. They invited me to the afternoon performance being held that day. I went, and it was very gratifying. That was my exclusive writing experience in the Army.

F: How was it gratifying, in what way?

E: Well, it was gratifying because it was the only thing I had written in all those years, and also because I got to see the live reaction to the sketch. It was just as I'd dreamed it would be; they roared at everything. I re-

member one joke in particular, these poor dirty slobs come
in right from the front, literally smelling, and one line was,
"The leaning tower of Pisa started leaning the other way."
I never expected this to happen. Just mailed it in and
thought I'd never hear about it again. Maybe he wouldn't
even use it . . . he said it was a real "stick out" sketch, the
best sketch in the show.

A: Can you remember how you felt as you were writing it?

E: No, I don't think so, we were out in some woods
someplace, and I just went over and sat down under a tree
and thought about it. I know I enjoyed it, the feeling of
writing again. When I got into the Army, my brother
pulled strings like mad trying to get me into the special
services, the entertainment section. Well, when I was
inducted and they asked me what I did for a living, I said I
was a joke-writer. The next thing I knew I was with the
Tank Destroyer Division. A lot of good that did! After a
while I was a combat soldier, and that was it for the rest of
the war. Later I wrote to my brother, "Aw, forget it." I got
to the point where I would have been embarrassed if I had
been taken out of there. Maybe it's dumb; but when you
think about it in retrospect, it's the front line soldier, it's a
certain kind of pride. What life becomes is living with the
men you're with and being able to look them in the eye. I
almost got myself killed a couple of times, but I was glad
when it was over that I could look the other guys in the
eye and say I did as much as they did. I think I would have
been really uncomfortable if I'd been jerked out for a "safe
job."

Then the War was over, and I got back to New York
and picked up where I'd left off. I was fortunate enough to
get a job with another columnist called Walter Kiernan. He
wrote topical jokes. He was a pretty big columnist. I got to
him because he was a friend of O'Keefe's. I was ghost-
writing for him. I'd read the papers every morning and see
what the crucial issues were, send him the jokes, he'd
print next day whatever he chose. My first really big break
was through O'Keefe. That's how the business goes, one
person tells another. Ed Wynn was coming to New York to

do the Texaco Star Theater. James Melton, the singer, was the star of it, and Wynn was to have a seven minute comedy spot. He was looking for writers, cheap writers, you know. He asked O'Keefe out in Hollywood if he knew anybody in New York. O'Keefe gave me a plug and I submitted some sample jokes to Ed Wynn. In those days, that's how you did it, speculative writing. Anyway, he liked the jokes and hired me. That lasted about twenty-six weeks, my first big job.

F: This was when?

E: Oh, about '45, maybe '46. Things were then pretty dead in New York, radio comedy had moved to Hollywood. Since all the comedians were out here, I decided to pack up and come out. I was still single at that time and my brother was doing very well out here. Through his contacts, I was able to get on the Jimmy Durante and Gary Moore radio shows. They were a team for awhile, and I got a job writing for Moore. He would come out and do a little opening monologue. Then he'd introduce Durante and they'd work together. It was my job to work on that opening monologue. That was the beginning of all the big things that happened to me. After Durante and Moore split up—that was their last year together as a team—I worked in subsequent years for each of them separately.

When television started, I went back to New York, to work for Gary Moore's daytime show. Durante had a once-a-month special and I worked on that, too, during the same period. I was very busy for that year and then the cable came in—you remember, all shows at that time had to originate in New York. When we got the cable, all the comedians flew like bees back to sunny California. It was still sunny in those days. We writers all came back here, too.

Then one thing led to another. I guess the best things that happened to me after those variety shows was situation comedy with the Danny Thomas show, "Make Room for Daddy." I've been with situation comedy ever since. During the last few years I gradually have gotten into production. This is what is happening to most of the writers at present. My whole career really started from my brother being in the business. If he hadn't been, God knows what I'd be today.

A: Maybe you'd have been funny, but not a writer?

E: Maybe, but how funny I'd be would depend on how good I'd be doing something else.

F: But that truly makes a lot of difference?

E: I think so. If something goes wrong personally, it can really throw me. It affects my concentration. Some guys can just go right on, but I'm not that type. I have to have a clear mind. I'm very neat and organized.

F: If something *does* interrupt you, do you have any special techniques for getting around it?

E: Just getting into the writing, I think that's the best medicine, losing myself in what I'm doing. My partner is incredible, in this way, he's incredible. Always has a brilliant and fresh mind whatever goes on. He just picks up where we left off the day before; he's much better at shutting other things out than I am. See, it's important, because in this business, you don't have time to wait for the best moment, to become inspired. It's not like you were a novelist and you could walk around for a year and suddenly an idea will hit you and you can wait for this inspiration. This becomes a business and it has to be more or less mechanical. We know that we have to do, for instance, twenty-six shows, twenty-six different scripts, for next season, and we start writing way back, we started four months ago.

F: Where do you and your partner work? And what time of the day?

E: We work normal hours. From 9:30 or 10:00 until 5:00 or 6:00, in this room or the other room, we each have separate offices. For the beginning we have a special apartment out at the boat Marina. We start our work for next season out there because it's much pleasanter than working here at the studio. Production hasn't started yet. The show isn't shooting, but we have to start preparing the scripts for the summer when shooting does begin. We just sit down and formulate a plan—what new elements can we inject into the series. You inject these new elements for two reasons, first, you want to keep it fresh, and, second, this gives you some angles for new stories. If you just don't change anything, you're going to run dry on story material. Then we plunge in and spitball ideas at first. We'll spend several days just saying: "Hey, how about doing a show where the dog gets lost and she has to go and try to find it?" We are, at this stage, just getting general notions, we don't go any further at that time. And then, after a few days, we'll zero in on what we've come up with, decide which ones will bear fruit. Then we'll pick maybe one-third of the ideas to continue.

F: Do you keep notes?

E: Oh, yes, we keep notes on all this.

F: Are you both actually writing at this time?

E: Well, the way we work, I write everything in long-hand on a legal pad—everything. When we eventually write the script, we work together line by line, right from the top, and I'll again write the entire script in longhand, it's really my own shorthand, only I understand it, then I translate it, dictate it to our secretary. Then she types it up for us. Before I had a secretary, I'd type it up myself, but now, I have a whiz of a girl, she is fantastic. Going back to the writing, we settle on whatever we think will work and then we develop these ideas into full stories. Some of them fall by the wayside; while you're in the act of developing them, you suddenly realize it won't work, that there's just not enough there. It's an elimination process and you end up with the best of what we originally thought of. When we have enough ideas, we meet with Doris (Doris Day, the star of the show) and let her in on what we're thinking so she won't be too surprised. We let her approve before we finish. When we have a batch of ideas, we start writing the scripts, one by one. This season we ourselves managed to write nine scripts before shoot-ing schedule. We bought six from outside writers, so we have fifteen so far. And, that's the actual mechanics of it all.

As far as what we go through mentally, how can I really describe it? It's a business, we can't afford to wait until tomorrow if we feel stale today. We have to do it today regardless, you know? It is a deadline situation. If we were writing a screenplay and there really were no deadline, and we had a bad day and weren't getting anywhere, we might have a tendency to say, "Let's forget it today and start fresh in the morning." Here, this is rare, because we just don't have the time.

A: When you're writing together in this final line-by-line period, how would you describe the state you're in most of the time?

E: Very intense. We shut ourselves off from everything. We happen to be two guys who, once we get rolling, can write very fast, as much as fifteen pages a day. Once we get rolling on a thing that's right, it's like a snowball going down a hill and gathering snow all the time, and at the end of it we're almost exhausted. It's a feeling like you've been jogging, it's like—*aaah!*—and you're spent. That's the way we work. A lot of others don't work quite as intensely. But we go in spurts. We'll have days when we won't get anywhere. Then the next day we'll go like maniacs. My partner is even more intense than I am. I'm the calm one, he's the pacer. He walks up and down like a caged lion and won't relax. I won't relax either, though I don't pace, until the day's work is done. We're very weary for awhile after we finish.

A: Are you very much dependent on each other for feedback along the way?

E: Yes, that's one of the important things out here. There are an awful lot of teams that write comedy, and you really have to be able to get along. It's even more crucial than a marriage because you spend more time with your partner than you do with your wife. You have to have a rapport and be able to feed each other without destroying each other. There grows an understanding after awhile, an understanding that if he pitches a line and I don't think it's funny, he can sense it. I don't have to say, "That's no good." We never use the words "great" or "good" in a negative way. If we don't say them right away, the other guy knows it hasn't been accepted, and tries something else. Once in awhile we'll make a fight for something we've thought of because we really think it is good and we'll try to talk the other into it. But we generally respect the rejection of the other. There are rejections and acceptances all day long, there have to be in a collaboration.

It's interesting, the different kind of routine you get into writing with someone else. Both my partner and I have worked alone in the past. That's another ball game because you don't have that opportunity to bounce it off another. You have to judge for yourself. You're really on your own. I would say that writing alone is harder, but probably when the work is done and it pays off, it's more rewarding, the feeling you've done it all yourself. There's nothing that can elate you more than that. The feeling of doing it well with another guy is also great, but it has been 50-50, so you can't take all the credit. The reason there are so many teams in comedy is this deadline pressure. You have to write fast, and on time. Writing alone I might take a week or two to complete a script, while working together we can knock one off every three or four days. When you have to do twenty-six shows, you do it to write faster.

A: Even in the collaboration situation, do you still get a residual feeling of high after completing what you think of as a good script? Something you carry around in you for awhile, or are you just immediately into the next script?

E: We're immediately into the next one. You can't even remember what you've written a few weeks before some of the time . . . all these scripts . . . The Production Manager will come in and say, "Hey, in the twelfth script, when they're out in the street, do you want to use a truck or a bus?" I'll say, "What street? What scene?" I don't even remember it. We get them out and go on to the next one. We dump each of them. It becomes an assembly line. Also we know we'll have to come back to it once we're in production. A week before each show shoots we have a production meeting and go over that script and refresh ourselves as to what it's all about. Maybe we do a little rewriting and cutting. There's no reason to stay emotionally with it after it's done. If anything, it's the reverse. I like to get rid of it and get onto the next.

A: So you are always in the middle of working. You don't have time for the usual rise and fall, the kind of natural easing-off, let-down folks usually experience after meeting a deadline. You're constantly building for the next.

E: That's right. In addition to our own scripts, we get those of other writers which we need to rewrite. When you're in this business, it's a continuing series of crises, like production where you'll get a scene that isn't working, or you need some better lines here, or there, things you can't anticipate before they happen, all these various mechanical things that have to be done and redone. So you don't always enjoy producing; it can be a drag. Outside of the writing, the only other truly creative part of the producing is the cutting. You are trained to know your audience, you should know what they'll laugh at.

There are laugh tracks available, so you can suggest it as funny as you want to. However, most of us writers come from a background where we know from experience what makes an audience laugh. Even with a laugh track, we'll say let's make believe it's real people. Well, it *is* real people out there. We have to be very careful to differentiate between what we like and what they will. You have to discard your own taste because you're really not writing to please yourself. If you're doing that, you should be doing a book or a play or whatever. This doesn't mean you have to write garbage, but you can't do ultra-sophisticated stuff either. This kind of writing is for the public, not for the writer himself.

Summary

The material from our interview with Jack Elinson gives rich detail on the states of *aloneness* and *togetherness*, as experienced by the humorist in his personal and professional lives.

We and you as readers—were witness to the Elinson dinner table with its "roaring laughter." Here the family,

gathered together in its communality (certainly an archetypal vision of the multiple-man state), fought off the
shadow of the Depression. Humor, said Jack, was
"somewhere in our blood." The family shared this gift for
"cracking up" one another. And yet, as evidence for that
ability to be in singular- and multiple-man states simultaneously, we clearly understand Jack's portrait of the
different types of humor created by different family members ("my father was the dry type, he had this sneaky
humor; very dry, very quiet"). And that humor, for each
member of the family was an individual experience and an
individual*ized* product.

There seem to have been two choices in the Elinson
clan: to carry on the family trade—as pharmacists; or to
carry out the family craft—as humorists.

As an avocation, Brother Izzy first began sending in
his gags to Winchell, became a professional at it, and this
helped to motivate and steer Jack in his direction. Starting
with Winchell, as the Elinson boys did, was one of the
traditional ways to be initiated into the humor business. A
great many of the well-known writers started in this way.
This introduction to the show-business route could be
passed on in the closeness of fraternity from Izzy to Jack.
As Jack put it, he wouldn't have become a writer if it
hadn't been for Izzy. Jack exhibits strong identification
with his "Will Rogers-like brother" and perhaps he would
have found it much easier to pursue pharmacology if it
hadn't been for his brother's becoming well-known as a
Winchell contributor. Such is the power of the family for
those who are part of close-knit clans. Many of us who
have had that familial tie search forever for a renewal of
such bonds, find it hard to *be* or to *do* alone.

As Jack told it, the climate of the Depression was
"panic." The family had to stick together for survival
purposes: "It was an automatic thing for a kid, the moment he could, to work and help support the family. That
was routine, there was nothing else to consider." And,
because of this, as he explains it, "money was . . . a big
thing, a driving force . . ," Therefore, when Izzy first left
his sure job at Borden's to go with Walter O'Keefe, the

unproven status of radio-gag-writing in that family caused a family crisis. Once Izzy became the equivalent of a millionaire in the strapped family, however, he had paved the way and Jack could go that route, too. With Mom as frugal as she was, it may have been easier for Jack.

The success of humor as a coping device is clearly indicated by the fact that, despite the tough times, Jack has such fond memories of the hysterical goings-on and the clowning in his family.

Jack's gag-writing career was interrupted by the war so that, in a sense, when the war was over he had to start all over again. Of special interest to us was the incident during the war when, for the first time in several years, Jack wrote his sketch based on Mauldin's Willie and Joe in a rest camp. Jack received great gratification when he saw his sketch performed, and heard for himself the roaring applause and laughter. This was certainly an instance of Jack's "going it alone," proving that he could write well alone and receiving that particular sense of gratification one gets because of the "feeling that you've done it all yourself." The incident gives a unique picture of the singular-man state. We can picture the young foot soldier, leaving his buddies, going off and sitting under a tree and thinking about his writing assignment—right in the middle of a war!

Jack speaks of his pride as a soldier—that he proved he could "do it as much as they did," and did not opt for a soft job in the Entertainment Division. In essence, Jack can always say he is the same as others, yet different—unique—himself.

After the war Jack seems to have been on a straight course; picking up where he'd left off. He admits that he more-or-less followed his brother's footsteps, successfully using his contacts, making it sound as if it had been a very easy process. Clearly, Jack didn't have to pound on doors. He was no solitary writer in Bohemia waiting for a patron to find him in his hermitic garret. Rather, we see a picture of an efficient young man who knew what he wanted and moved straight toward his goal. By this we certainly mean no reflection on Jack's creative talent. As we see with

Arnie Rosen and in much of Ruth Flippen's interview the same sense of: "this is the way it's done, and now that I've learned how, I'm getting on with it."

The office in which we interviewed Jack had the look of organization and efficiency. But, over and above that was the touch of poignance in the way Jack talked of his boyhood years and of his large family, and his yearning when expressing the hopelessness he sometimes feels about crossing the generation gap with his own kids.

Jack fits into the category of the "non-performing" writer. He projects the image that he isn't always "on," that he doesn't crave that kind of attention. His style is more restrained; he is a private person. Yet, it is possible to interpret that much of his childhood clowning at the dinner table was skillfully structured and acted out in his collaborative writing efforts in later years.

A master of situation comedy, Jack has been captive to the deadline. He *had* to be disciplined, and to develop a method for making sure that each script could be plucked out of the typewriter on time. There was simply no time to play at the romance of "inspirational" writing.

A moving part of our interview came when Jack discussed how he is not the kind of person who just laughs and chuckles through life. "If something goes wrong personally, it can really throw me," he said. He doesn't have the automatic "the show must go on" personality.

So, the multiple-man state of writing is an essential part of Jack's professional life. But also, his mind must be clear and he must be free of distractions in order to get on with his work. His partner "in the marriage of writing" is great at this, he admits—"much better at shutting out other things than I am."

Jack produces tremendous insights into the "business of the Business" as he graphically tells what it's like to do 26 scripts a season. He and his partner have a highly-structured, well-oiled machine which, as he tells it—seems to just spew out the scripts. Yet, we know that the functioning of this assembly line is dependent upon the quick associations and the inventiveness of the assem-

bly line "workers." It may seem pat, but we all understand
there is nothing pat about it at all.

We picture Jack and his partner flowing between
their singular and multiple states continuously. This facility of transition has been achieved, perhaps, by endless
run-throughs, and because of sustained drive. They have
a master plan; they have made it work in the past; they
have reaped the rewards of success; they believe in themselves and they jump right in again. They know what will
work; they are able to eliminate what will not. They
balance each other well; they know each other's reactions
so intimately.

There is a great deal of mutual reinforcement in the
interaction. It *is* like a marriage in that the dependency and
intimacy is mutual; they are necessary to one another's
well-being. As Jack says, the feedback is a necessity . . .
"You have to have a rapport and be able to feed each other
without destroying each other." They have learned non-
punitive ways of eliminating the other's material when
they do not feel it's good enough. As Jack says, there is a
"certain understanding," and he doesn't ever have to say,
"That's no good." They seem to have achieved an ideal
state of both commonality and communality; they are
sharing and able to accept both rejections and acceptances
from each other. Such is the highest potential of the state
of togetherness.

And, through their mutual accomplishments—even
when dealing with traditional formulae or situations
—each of them, as individuals, can triumph to the extent
that Jack reports a high level of intense, steaming surges of
feeling when things are going well.

The sadness in Jack's report comes in his having to
cultivate an emotional distance from each script. This is a
very different "style of creating" from that described by
Billy Barnes, for instance, but it is a style that has worked
and worked well for Jack. One has to admire this kind of
performance under extreme pressure.

To attempt to judge creativity on the basis of what
manner of creating is most valid or virtuous would be
counterproductive. The "creator" is not some generalized

person. All creators do not live the same life-style, nor maintain all of the same goals or values. And there is no reason that the professional creator, whether his field is humor or tragedy, should create in the same manner as does another.

So we risk the prediction that Jack Elinson—who first sent his material to Winchell in his teens—will create, in solitude and in union with others, for all of his life, even though he may never act out his ideas for his friends, nor ever announce again the significance and meaning of writing in the entire course of his life.

Ruth Brooks Flippen

The Relationship of Creativity to
Internal and External Reinforcement

RUTH BROOKS FLIPPEN was born in Brooklyn and was graduated from Northwestern University in 1943. Her professional writing career began right after that. She wrote that she did not include her birthdate "not because she was sensitive about age or anything like that, but was just following the old show business saying, 'always leave them wanting just a little bit more.'"

A superb writer of situation comedy, she has written enormously and successfully for such shows as "That Girl," "The Sandy Duncan Show," and "Bewitched," among others. Her most recent work has been movies for television, notably, "Baby, Baby, Baby" which was up for an Emmy.

"I have a 'thing' about having my picture taken," she wrote when we asked for a picture. "I'm afraid the one I'm enclosing is the only decent one I have. Incidentally, I'm the blonde . . . the brunette is one of my cats."

Long after this book has gone to press, we shall have an indelible image of a scene we never saw in real life—but so vivid in memory that it seems as if we had been there. This is the picture of Ruth Flippen in her first stage appearance.

"I got my first laugh when I was three years old when I came out on the stage with a big black shawl over my head, leaned up against the podium and sang, 'It cost me a lot, but there's one thing that I've got—my man . . .' The audience laughed. I didn't know why, but I figured as long as they were laughing, I might as well pursue it."

One doesn't have to be a soothsayer to figure out what happened to little Ruth after that instantaneous successful debut. No matter how precocious she may have seemed to the audience, she really had no idea what it really meant to have "her man." She was not Fanny Brice at three. She was not Fanny Brice onstage or off of it. She was a little girl who had learned to imitate a routine that was "in" at the time. She played it to the hilt, brought down the house; she liked the feeling of it, so she decided she'd try it again.

Such is the power of *social reinforcement*—the label psychologists have for the "goodies" we get from other people. This need is considered a secondary one, as compared to a primary or inborn need. Learning theorists explain quite readily how this takes place. A child is born. If healthy, he has an instinct to suck. Sucking is so instinctual that the baby will suck on just about anything that goes into his mouth. He also needs to eat and his means to fulfill that need is the sucking instinct, and the tendency to cry from "hunger-pain" if a parent doesn't arrive before the hunger begins to hurt. Learning theorists

71

would point to that primitive moment of the child crying out for food, then pleasantly sucking and being relieved as providing the key to subsequent development of the young individual to society. According to them, social development comes about through the eventual ability of a child to separate the image of his "feeding other" from his own image. Later, associations are projected from the one or two recognized others to all "that-is-not-baby," and eventually, the young infant creates his own categorization of "those-who-are-familiar-to-me" and "those-who-are-not." These simple concepts are basic to an understanding of the process of socialization and represent the nucleus from which the idea of social reinforcement issues.

In this vein, we approach the story of Ruth Flippen. The fact that she was a child star offers an ideal opportunity to observe social reinforcement—the importance of parents and family and friends and audiences.

Psychologist F. Allport made an important contribution about the importance of "others" in the learning process in 1924 that is germaine to our discussion here. A parent may directly participate in the teaching of a child, his presence being essential to the learning process. An entire continuum of participation of social "others" in the learning of the child (or an adult, for that matter) exists. At one end is direct participation; at the other end of the continuum there is presence or implied presence of a parent (a parent watching a child perform, for example). Allport called this *social-facilitation*. Even in non-direct participation of a parent, a child recongizes what his parent wants him to do and what will bring him rewards or affection, etc., and so tends to behave in these ways.

We may never be certain whether little Ruth became proficient in her routine by seeing someone else do it many times, by being instructed in doing it by her mother, or because she happened to see the routine done once, tried it out and was then urged to do it again by her family. What we do know and what you discover in her interview, was how wrapped up her parents were in her being a "show biz kid." This was true to the point where her mother often sang her songs with her and did her bits with her. Little Ruth was not born singing "My Man" and smiling coyly out of her black shawl. Somewhere along the line, there was some imitation or identification which, in turn, was rewarded. If not, little Ruth would never have climbed onto that stage and become Baby Ruth.

Julian Rotter's social learning theory will be helpful to us here, especially considering the phenomenon of the show biz kid—the kind that Ruth Flippen eventually became—a child who was center-stage both onstage and off. Rotter's theory departs from those of other behaviorists and learning theorists in that he specifies two different kinds of environments: one that is meaningful to the individual, and one that is not. The meaningful environment has power over the individual as it contains a set of cues that arouse the individual's expectations. If he does *this*, he will get *that*; if he does not, he may get something else.

When little Ruth ended her song and received laughs and applause, that external reinforcement caused the stage setting to become a meaningful environment for her. It became one of the major psychological elements in her life. She learned to expect that, if she used her repertoire of funny, imitative behaviors, she would receive rewards.

When a child is very young, external factors are extremely important to him, both because he is so dependent on adult figures to "keep him alive," and because he is not able yet to depend upon himself to self-motivate activities other than the basic ones of eating and sleeping.

Social learning theorists agree that the need for responses such as praise, respect, attention are *acquired*. They also feel that secondary responses rapidly become as important to individuals in our culture as the primary ones. We should remember that if one has a great need for recognition, the referent for that need is external.

Rotter's theories are important to us in yet another way. He was interested in individual personality differences related to whether or not a person is directed largely toward obtaining internal or external reinforcement. Does an individual do what he does because he is aware of and satisfied with his power to reinforce himself? Or does he do so to get the respect, praise, and applause of others? This is something we could ask about all of our writers—or about any artist or creator, for that matter.

Relevant to this internal-external dichotomy is the matter of the two types of writer-life-styles. On one side, the writer continuously creates, invents, and even performs while he lives. He enjoys the attention he gets and, like Herbie Baker, enjoys being the life of the party. On the other side, we find the more subdued type, who, although enjoying humor, does not play it out for the public and can be satisfied inside of himself with his own evaluation of his material.

The first kind of creator responds strongly to the reassurance of others. The second type of creator responds most strongly to the creative act itself—what he experiences internally and over which he exercises control.

Learning theorist Albert Bandura demonstrates that a child may develop without the ability to reinforce himself in a positive way, if he has had adult models with such stringent demands on themselves that they never felt deserving of positive reinforcement. Such a child could become self-punitive or self-denigrating. Bandura believes that low self-esteem grows out of not living up to expectations which are not realistic, either one's own expectations or those of adult models.

The recent trend toward interest in selfreinforcement and self-control is especially interesting because, for many years, the staunch American psychological academic group would not even use words beginning with "self." Now some leading behaviorists are free with the word, believing now that self-reinforcement works and perhaps is even essential to such therapeutic interventions as quitting smoking or drinking. They are even extending the "self" concept with another word that was formerly a huge "no-no": will-power. This represents a small group of social scientists who are nimbly crossing the great divide between humanistic and behavioristic psychology.

These people argue that, to have self-reinforcement as a basic part of one's behavior, the person in question must like himself; must have experienced control over his environment and must have goals which are attainable and clear in mind. Bandura summed it up well: the person with a good self-concept will believe that he has enough control over his environment to perform well and to change things. Someone incapable of operating under his own system of reinforcement is likely to feel that whether he does "anything" or "nothing," life will be the same.

Another theory offered by Rotter has significance in our study of creative people. He claims there is a continuum of internal-external control upon which people find themselves. People on the external end of the scale feel that the environment more or less controls them and reinforcement contingencies do *not* depend on their own actions, but are afforded them by chance. These people lead restricted lives and have very low expectancies that anything they do will change the outcomes or consequences of their behavior.

People on the internal end of the control scale tend to feel that what they do *does* result in reinforcement, and they do not feel that the environment is in control of their destinies.

The significance of these theories to creative people should be fairly obvious. Creative people must be alone a great deal of the time. If they feel that what they do has little connection with what results, they tend to produce stale, formula kind of work. They get little satisfaction from their work and they believe that external forces provide them with their satisfaction, no matter what they write. In a studio setting, such people are less likely to take an active part in story conferences, feeling that the "powers that be" will determine what's in the script, anyway.

There is also significant relevance of internal and external reinforcement for creativity and the process of creating. The writer who works alone must be able to sustain himself through difficult moments without tension-reducing or rewarding external experiences. Some writers cannot write two pages without reading them to someone (or telephoning someone even with the germ of an idea to get response on whether or not it's "really good.") These people are highly oriented to external reinforcement. Writers with this orientation have a hard time making it through long-term projects such as writing film scripts, and need to repeatedly leave the typewriter or tape recorder to perform for wife or agent. These people also feel themselves to be judged by the public's reaction to their work rather than a personal, gut-level feeling about the quality of the work.

Earlier in this section we referred to the effects of modeling on a child's feeling about himself and his worth. What parents do in reaction to a child's behaviors, how much they expect of a child, when and how he is rewarded—all of these things give the child expectations about the reinforcements he will get from the world, and impressions regarding his own abilities and limitations. These parental moves help to establish the entire pattern of gestalt or self-esteem for their child.

Only with true self-esteem can we believe in our ability to effect changes in our environment. Only by succeeding in gaining internal satisfaction on our own will we stay internally-motivated.

Ruth Flippen's interview is a natural and spontaneous illustration of an individual's fluctuation between internal and external controls. We see her development from being an externally-motivated child singing "My Man" because she was told to do so even though she really didn't understand what it was all about—to becoming a behind-the-scenes, problem-solving writer who isn't afraid to put in her two cents worth and to work —strategically—for the points she wants.

Family therapists like Jay Haley and Salvador Minuchin, and psychiatric anthropologists like Jules Henry have described beautifully the nature of stereotypic roles in the setting of the family. Ruth Flippen held a crucial and fixed role in her family group. Her awareness of this, her ability to use it eventually for her benefit, and to transcend her dependency on others for motivation and for reinforcement is a significant life-study.

Interview

R. Flippen: I was born in Brooklyn—you've probably heard *that* one before.

Fry: And how did you get into the business?

RF: Well, actually, I was pushed into show business when I was three years old. I was always being pushed into the Business and into Comedy.

F: By whom?

RF: By everybody. I got my first laugh when I was three years old when I came out on the stage with a big black shawl over my head, leaned up against the podium, and sang:

"It cost me a lot, but there's one thing that I've got—my man . . ."

The audience laughed. I didn't know why, but I figured as long as they were laughing, I might as well pursue it!

So I became Baby Ruth—that was the whole style at the time. If you couldn't find Sutter's gold, you put your child into show business. That's the way you got rich before the Jackie Coogan law. I sang and danced and I was over the hill by the time I was six. There was a new baby on the bill who was only four, you know?

F: And where was that first performance?

RF: In the New England area, in New London.

F: In what sort of theater?

RF: One that was dying. They were running acts in between motion pictures. Obviously, I wasn't much of a hit, because you probably never heard of me, but my name was like the candy bar, Baby Ruth. I had a marvelous poster:

Baby Ruth Tonight! Free Spaghetti!

F: Were either your mother or father in show business?

RF: No, nobody in the family was. As a matter of fact, my grandmother, whose maiden name was Bach, got very nervous when I was around six, because I was getting local publicity. Everybody was saying, "Where did this little child come from?" But, to tell you the truth, I don't think it was really talent, I was more like a chimpanzee. I learned how to imitate and do cute things. I'm digressing, but I think this is a hang-up with all former child performers. You're put up there on the stage; you're taught that approval is important; at first, you don't know how or why you're getting it, but you know somehow that it's part of the love and approval you need to get from your parents. And, you know, it's kind of awful when you *don't* get a hand, or when people laugh at you and you don't even know why. This kind of thing happens particularly when you begin to get gangly and aren't so cute anymore and all those little clever things don't work so well, so you always keep searching to get a hand again. I think maybe that's what develops the comic senses. You're either going to get a laugh or you're going to cry a lot. So that, even in my early years, I was always prepared to make a joke. I tried to turn everything into a joke.

F: In your home? With your friends?

RF: Yes.

F: In school?

RF: Yes. *Everywhere.*

Allen: Were you an only child?

RF: Obviously. I had uncles who at fifteen and sixteen were sent to bed at nine, but I was allowed to stay up until 11 or 12! I was very precocious, and really just a horrible child. I wouldn't *have* a child like that in my own home.

My Grandmother (on the Bach side) was finally pinned down about what was making her nervous and she confessed she thought she was the Cassandra of Johann Sebastian Bach, that he had 26 children, but the thing that was making her nervous was that thirteen of those children were illegitimate, and she didn't know *which* branch she came from. She was afraid that if it ever came out that *I* was from the illegitimate branch, it would ruin my career in show business. But she thought that was where the talent came from.

A: That would have been fantastic publicity!

RF: You *know*, things *have* changed, and Boop Boopy Do *does* figure in with Bach and counterpoint now.

F: And you mentioned that there was quite a bit of music in your presentations.

RF: Yes, at that time I was doing singing, dancing, and anything else that small children do. Lots of imitations —with "My Man," I was obviously trying to do the Fanny Brice thing. "Brother, can you spare a dime" got a big laugh, too, you know, and "Sophisticated lady." I had a knack for choosing them. I sang for my grammar school and they sat there looking absolutely stunned, because they didn't even know what the songs meant! Neither did *I!*

But, I chose those songs and routines myself and, like most child performers, I got more and more courageous. This was also true as my writing career developed later. But I feel I was a lot more courageous when I was younger than I am now. When I was six years old and moved to Hartford, they had a big radio program on WTIC and I was supposed to sing on that show. I had a big argument with the manager because he didn't want me to sing the verse, and I eventually won. I sang the verse. As I say,—where angels fear to tread. When you're young, and don't know any better, you demand; then when you're older, you demand less, particularly in *this* business.

A: Originally, though, like when you sang, "My Man," who conceived of that kind of act?

RF: Well, actually, the first song I *ever* sung was "Ain't She Sweet," a typical thing. Evidently I had a flare for the dramatic, playing things very large, even as a kid, so I guess maybe I dug the Pagliacci bit, singing things beyond my years. I always sang the sad things, supposedly fraught with meaning, but I didn't have a very good voice. I really wasn't a very good dancer either, although I *did* teach dancing after I—through the bad years, the Depression, and its wake.

Most of my performances then were what they called club-dates. I would leave high school at two in the afternoon and go to Barrington, Vermont, a drive of three or four hundred miles, to sing and dance, usually on a bill with strippers on it. They really didn't care *how* they exposed kids then. I remember, for instance, that I was eight years old when I was first put on a bill with a stripper. To tell you how long ago that was, we called it Armistice Day. I can remember it so well, it was an Elk's Club thing, and this woman went on before me in some kind of a strange dress, and sang "If I could be with you one hour tonight." It was what we used to call cabaret singing. She went around and sat on the men's laps and laughed, and they were all grabbing at her, and they were drunk, you know. Even at that age, when I couldn't even understand what she was doing, all I was thinking of was how in the hell would I follow her! I was thinking I was afraid to sing "Here's the Key to My Heart" and pass out keys, or "Tie a Little String Around your Finger." I knew I was going to bomb and I *did*.

F: What a combination!

A: What are your memories about what was happening inside of you in those days? Do you remember how you felt?

RF: I felt a great discrimination against us, against me in the degree that I still have hangups about it. I was thrown out of church—like Debbie Reynolds. I loved church, I was a Methodist, and I used to love Sunday School. However, when they found out that I was singing and dancing at night, they wouldn't let me go, so I began going to my girl friends' churches. I'd go to the Catholic Church one week, then a synagogue the next. Because of that, I got a really marvelous overall sense of a liberal kind of religion, which was unusual in those days. But, also because of that, I always had a terrific hangup. That because I was in show business, I was slightly less than everyone else, do you see? My husband used to tell about a period even before I was born when they used to have signs on boarding houses saying: "No Dogs or Actors."

A: I know. My father acted in Chautauqua Society as a teenager and he used to tell that same story. In the deep South, especially.

RF: In school, I wasn't able to date or do the normal kind of childhood things, because I was working all the time and I always felt apart and different. Also, they would inevitably call upon me to do a show for school and *that* set me further apart. I hated that. I wasn't able to be part of the group. The only way I was able to fit in any group at all was to be with older people, which in some ways accounts, I guess, for my later marrying Jay, who was a great deal older than I. That was the pattern I followed. In many ways, I looked upon Jay as a father.

F: You lived in Brooklyn until you were five? And then?

RF: We moved to New London, to what is now called Uptonville, Connecticut, and then later to Hartford.

F: Who lived with you in New London?

RF: My mother, my father, and my paternal grandparents. Also my dad's three brothers and sister.

F: All together?

RF: At that time, yes, they were all in the house.

A: You had a large audience!

RF: *Yes indeed,* but it was a miracle that they ever liked me, because of what I told you. Here were the brothers, all sent to bed, strictly disciplined. They heard—Don't speak unless you're spoken to—and I was always allowed to "be on."

There was also a terrific tug-of-war between my mother and father over me. In retrospect, my father was *right.* I needed more balance; he was always trying to filter me down, whereas my mother was always trying to push me further.

F: She was the one who was most interested in your career then?

RF: He was, too, but he wanted me to—

F: Have other experiences.

RF: Yes. At least, he wanted me to be kept in my place. He used to call me "Madame Queen."

F: Where do you think this inclination to push came from in your mother?

RF: Probably out of total frustration.

F: Did she have natural talents that weren't developed?

RF: She obviously *thought* so because she used to learn all my routines with me, sing along, and tell me when to smile. As a matter of fact, I think it was a tremendous disappointment to her that I became a writer because that was an area she does not understand *and* I think she felt I fell below the mark. In some ways it was a compensation for her that Jay was an actor, I feel, because that was the part of show business she liked. She so wanted to be a part of it, the fans, the autographs, the limelight. When I married Jay, she really identified, although she never wanted to be called his mother-in-law, or Mom. She *loved* being with celebrities, meeting them, being a part of it all, and I think even today she kind of wishes I had kept on my original path and had become a star.

The writing end of it she doesn't dig at all, *but*, only a year ago, she decided to try it. She went to Spain and wrote a journal. When she came back, she wanted me to read it.

A: So she eventually tried your trade again, like when she sang along with you as a kid? Kind of a vicarious thing?

RF: This happened all along, the vicarious thing. Especially since Jay died, I've made it very plain to her that we are not going to be the Dolly Sisters anymore. For instance, I called her Brooksie. My maiden name is Brooks, and by the time I was 18, I got so fed up with going through a department store and trying to pick out a dress and saying, "Mother, do you like this?" Then the salesgirl would say, "Oh, is that your mother? You look like sisters." Obviously, I was rebelling against the vicarious thing. Father had died, and so I decided to call her Brooksie.

F: Did she have an occupation of her own?

RF: Well, by the time I got into dancing school, she made all the costumes, and she got into that, she was very good at that. Then, after my father died, she went back to her original sideline, being a switchboard operator, and she worked at the Fuller Brush Company until recently when she had to retire. Part of that frustration for show business paid off at the switchboard because they all thought she was just marvelous. She's always very sweet and cute on the phone, the kind of old-fashioned super service that doesn't exist much anymore.

My father was a hotel clerk. I guess he tried everything. Actually, his real occupation was being a Disabled
War Veteran. Show business was part of his hang-up, too.
He would have loved to have been Mike Todd. I say that
because he was the kind of guy who, if he had 50 cents in
his pocket, 45 of it was for a tip. He was a big man. He
desperately wanted that identification, but things just got
progressively worse for him. In those days, in order to be
eligible for any pension at all, he had to be pronounced
totally disabled. Then, of course, he couldn't do *any* kind
of work. From that time on, it was just a dying process
—between the booze and also the constant conflict between my mother and him fighting over me. They differed
on how I should be raised and how I shouldn't be raised,
what I was to do and not to do. The horrible thing was my
working when *he* couldn't and my mother working when
he couldn't. She kind of rubbed it in, too, with, I guess,
some justification, but it was really kind of sad. By the
time I got to college, he had one last bout with all of this,
ended up in the hospital, and finally died. I think originally they were going to call the cause, "Alcoholism," but
they were kind about it and said it was a heart attack.
F: With all of the conflict and disappointment you're
telling us about, what part do you remember humor
playing in your household?
RF: Well, I think it was a natural defense for me. From
the beginning, I turned all the dreadful things that happened to me into funny stories. I guess I was afraid people
might "find out." The fights were terrible; they were
sometimes physical, and very bad—you could hear
them—I knew other people could hear them. It was a very
poor area in Hartford, not quite tenement houses, but
close apartments, and one family always knew when
another family was fighting, or a husband came home
drunk, or a wife was thrown out in the street in the middle
of the night. From the very beginning, I learned that the
best way to go was to tell a funny story before anybody
came back and told the same material to you as a tragic
story. I guess I did it by instinct and always have. Sometimes it *can* be a hangup. Recently I went through a heavy
period and finally had to go to a shrink. I started right out

by telling him all these hysterically funny stories, like "my father once hit me in the mouth" and he said, "What's so funny?" That was the first realization I ever had that these stories were really not as funny as I was trying to make them. That it was a defensive thing. Still, despite the fact I am now aware of it, I'll usually go for the laugh every time.

A: Are you aware when you do this? Is it deliberate or automatic?

RF: It comes as natural to me as an accent, as speech rhythms, as whatever your body language is, particularly when you've started out that young. I've been told I have a comic delivery. I know this is true even when I'm writing, for example, I have to act the thing out. That's where I find out if it's going to get a laugh—I try it. I really am still a frustrated actress. Many times I'll say something outrageously funny. Oh, I always hear myself after I've said it, and usually know it was outrageous or whatever, and I'll laugh myself, but I have to say it first.

This is one thing I've learned to discipline myself about, slightly anyway, not entirely, as you'll see if you listen to tapes of my story conferences. With men, you always have to be kind of careful not to hurt masculine feelings and pride, you know, but there are times when you get pushed to the wall and the hostility builds up and you can't resist . . . you go for the line and the laugh, and then apologize later. But I feel that's a bad thing and I shouldn't do it.

A: So sometimes you are holding back, but finally you just can't take it any longer, and you pull the plug. When you deliver that line do you feel like you're testing things out to see what's going to happen?

RF: Well, I guess it's a little like one-upmanship. You take so much, that you finally have to show you're not really all that stupid. I don't know if men feel the same way—they might describe it differently, but in these television show story conferences, particularly on what they call the committee shows, you have to please so many people. You'll get a story editor who has to interpret what everybody else wants, and they have told you what they want, and you have written it that way. Now they want to rewrite, and you find they've all changed their minds. But they have to put it on the basis of "This just isn't *right*," and they forget that it's exactly what they *asked* you to do. So it becomes very degrading and you begin to feel like you imagine a whore must feel. You've really been used, and you've got to get some dignity somewhere along the line, even if it's only to get in one side remark here or there. Many times I can get it out in the script itself, then you've done what they wanted you to do, but you held onto a little of your own self respect.

A: I guess the thing I was basically aiming at in asking you: is it sometimes bigger than just trying for a laugh?

RF: Yes, it's, at least on one level, ego-saving. Male or female, in freelancing for television, you have to keep reminding yourself of your worth, your values, your talent, because many times the people with whom you're working are not creative people. They come at you with lines and instructions like for Sandbox "A." And often you find yourself meekly saying, "Oh, yes, that's fine, that's great," or whatever. As a matter of fact, since I've started to go back to school (*Note:* Ms. Flippen had entered USC in the graduate program), I have thought of writing some kind of paper just on the story conference itself, the kinds of lines that are used in it. I've made several relevant notes.

There are some typical kinds of clichés that go into story conferences when the producers are feeling their way—trying to get what they want into the story. It's like play acting, or a game. It's like a husband and wife trying to buy a house. You find out how easy it is to get a divorce, if you're trying to buy a house! That's really where it's at. *And*, all of a sudden, you find out whole new things about each other that you didn't know existed before. Why all of a sudden does he have to have a yard? When you have a story conference, you get the same kinds of little clues, little stimuli.

A: You seem very intrigued with and very insightful about the writing process?

RF: I had good teachers, at Northwestern. By the time I got into high school, I was directing shows, and putting them on. I didn't even realize I was writing then, but suddenly the Dean of Girls decided I should go to college. That was out of the realm of my wildest dreams; besides, I hadn't prepared for it. But she worked out a plan whereby she would help me, loan me money, and I would work my way through. Her idea was for me to go to college and become a director. I went to Northwestern, and in my second year, my advisor, who was a wonderful man and a frustrated writer, suggested I take a writing course, because in order to become a writer (he said), you had to *learn* how to become a writer.

Since I was working my way through school and paying back the loan, it was just too heavy a schedule. You had to write for radio class a half-hour script each week, and that was thirty-five pages. I kicked; I screamed; I hollered. But, he forced me to take the course, and the second week, he said, "Forget it, you're already a writer." From then on, I concentrated on my writing and I was very fortunate, because as soon as I graduated, I went to work at NBC, on network radio. I started on staff and graduated to a comedy show.

I had great advice all the way through. My professor, Al Crews, and Max Wiley, who was a radio writer, always said: "When you're writing something, never talk about it, never tell anybody about it until you've put it down on paper, because, if you do, it's like giving the performance. You will have received the applause already, then when it comes to write the stuff, it's like after-the-fact. You will have lost the enthusiasm—that marvelous thing of having to get it all down."

That's part of what happens in these story conferences. By talking and playing things out, it's like the show has been done and, all of a sudden, they decide they don't like it because the one who's performing it is the associate producer, and, as Fred Allen said, "You know who an associate producer is, he's the only man who will associate with a producer." There's always one little guy in the room who comes up with *such* gems, like "Why don't you get a foot caught in a bowling ball?" He's there to give the producer confidence.

A: Is there another side of the coin? Several writers we've talked with mention the positive aspects about "teaming," the response you can get from playing off the other guy. Can it be positive for *you* as well as negative?

RF: Well, here's a strange story that is relevant. When I started at NBC, I had as my first commercial job writing a comedy show for Billie Burke, which I was supposed to do in collaboration with Johnny Lund, who was a writer at that time. Just when we began, he got offered a part in "The Hasty Heart" and he turned actor. I was left to do this half-hour show all alone which was incredible because they always had men in teams writing it previously, but they never got around to getting me a partner. Since then I have always worked alone. Strangely enough, come to think of it, I can't recall *any* women writing-teams. The women I know who write, write alone. Maybe a collaboration came along after the first script was done, or something. I do know of one lady writer who usually ends up working in collaboration, but most of the women who actively write for television comedy write alone. So it's mostly men who end up in teams. I don't think this really has to do so much with writing itself as with the inherent loneliness of the Business. Again, I'm only guessing, but I think that women are better able to cope with that than men.

In my case, I have a particular hangup that relates to the advice I told you about before. Other writers customarily share their work. They call other writers, or friends, ask for advice, or for opinions. I don't know where I got the idea, but I always thought of that as *cheating.*

I've at least now progressed to the point where I can call the producer and say—Look, I can't handle this, I've got a problem from here to here—Since it's their show, I can do that. But when I'm working on something of my own I still feel like I'm cheating if I ask somebody else about it.

A: Do you think this might possibly come out of the fact that you actually took writing *classes*, which is unusual for most writers. You actually had to turn things in as assignments you did work alone originally *and* you had it suggested to you NOT to talk things out.

RF: Yeah, that could have something to do with it, but I also think it goes back to the confusion of "nos" from my parents, to not being sure of what was right and what was wrong.

F: Childhood influences?

RF: Mostly personal, yes. The normal thing for writers is to call another writer and say, "Help, I'm having a problem. I'm great on the receiving end, but when I ask for help, well, that's part of my whole personal thing. I feel I mustn't ask for help.

F: Can you give us a brief runthrough of how your career out here developed?

RF: Well, Billie Burke wanted me to come out here. The Mazie show was on radio then with Ann Sothern and I also did a few of those. Because of that, I got a contract at Warner Brothers as a film-writer. I hadn't the faintest idea of how to do that. I worked for about a year there, did some scripts, but nothing came out of them. They dropped my option. Eventually, after looking at an original of mine, MGM hired me. I had a funny call from my agent. He said that MGM was calling and was interested. They wanted to know how much I weighed and how tall I was! I said, I'm a writer, what does *that* have to do with anything?

I did a few pictures there and went to Columbia where I eventually got involved in the Gidget series. By that time, television was moving along. I went to the Gidget series on TV and then became story editor on "Bewitched." Later, I joined "That Girl" in that capacity—which was a delight. I loved story editing, working with young writers, and that's one of the reasons I've gone back to school. Someday, I'd like to teach. But story-editing in and of itself is a backbreaking and thankless job. You work from 7:30 in the morning until 11 or 12 at night and all through the weekend. You can get called down to the set because they need a line "right now" at any moment. There is just no let-up.

On that show, I originated the idea of putting conferences on tape because Danny (Arnold) is such a marvelous ad-libber. He can ad lib a story just as he looks at
you. We were losing a lot of these great stories, so I
thought we could get them on tape. The story-editor has
problems playing both ends off against the middle. You
have to guide the writer along the line of what is needed,
while satisfying the specific things the producers want on
the show, the kinds of things the star wants which work
best for him or her, etc.

Then when the first draft comes in, you meet again
with everybody. Maybe for reasons that have nothing to
do with the quality of the script, changes have to be made.
It may be that you've gone over budget and that you just
cannot play a scene outside, no matter *how* funny it is.
There are so many reasons why things have to be
changed. The miracle is not that it gets on the air and is
good; the miracle is that it gets on the air at *all.* And I think
the basic thing a writer has to learn is that when somebody
says, "I don't like this line," it doesn't mean, "I don't like
you." Some writers never learn this. They still take that
deeply and personally as an affront.

F: What kind of planning is involved? How far ahead
do you stay? Or perhaps how far behind can you be is a
better question.

RF: You're all over the place. Sometimes you're half
ahead with the script that's shooting. But this afternoon
they might need that changed scene I told you about, so
you've got to do that. Or maybe the theme doesn't work,
and they're waiting right on the set for you. As story
editor, you have an office right there, you're part of the
production unit, and you really *live* there. You never go
out to lunch, you're always eating those rotten sand-
wiches from the Canteen and working through dinner. An
Ernie Kovacs picture I worked on was already in production when they called me to rewrite it. They got me a
dressing room with a typewriter in it. I was there at seven
o'clock in the morning and rewrote what they were going
to shoot. When they were ready to shoot, at nine a.m., I

would run in with the pages. It was really an insane job. That was when I learned that you don't wait for the famous electric light bulb to come on. You just *do* it. It has to be done and it has to be funny.

F: How does that feel? What do you go through emotionally?

RF: It's like housework. It has to be done; the goddamn dust is on the table and it's got to be cleaned off. As a matter of fact, it's probably very good that's the way it is.

F: You develop a total concentration.

RF: Right. A lot of people say you can't teach writing. Well, I don't think that's true. I think that if somebody wants to be an acrobat, well, sure it helps if they're double-jointed. But, if they're not, there are ways to teach people to do a walk-over or a back-spin.

There are basic things you can teach them that will help them if they want to work on the exercises, if they want to get limber enough, and if they have enough of that one little thing that gets them going. The same thing applies to writing—there *are* basic rules.

When you're in trouble with a script and a scene won't work, try writing it backwards. Or take the lines the girl is saying and give them to the boy—for that matter take an old joke and switch it. That, of course, is a basic key to comedy writing. There are maybe eight basic jokes in comedy and you simply learn how to switch them: "Who was that lady I saw you with last night?"

"That was no lady; that was my brother; he walks that way."

F: You're bringing in some very important material. Where did such knowledge, of techniques, etc. originally come from?

RF: Originally, it is instinct. The first script I wrote for Professor Crews made him decide that I was to be a comedy writer. Writers are typecast just as actors are. I tried to write a serious piece and these comments came back, "Boy, is this funny. It's murder."

It was always instinct with me. Or osmosis. I was on bills with long-time professionals and I was always watching professionals, watching them instead of relating to kids my own age. I didn't learn to play childhood games. I was learning the professional game. You know, I put on shows of my own to help send other kids to camp. I didn't know that I should have been sent to camp. Even in dancing, it was a question of pacing and timing. Some of it is instinctive, but also osmosis. If you're in that arena, it's seeping into you. I can still do a shimmy if necessary.

A: Are there any rules about rhythm in the construction of humour?

RF: Oh, yes, very definitely. One of the problems with dealing with non-creative producers is that in many cases they are not aware of how important rhythm and pacing are. There is a producer, who shall be nameless, who is known as a joke killer, for the very reason that he will make you rewrite: "Who was that lady I saw you with . . ." something like: "That was no lady, that was my darling, dear, sweet adorable wife." And there it lays—it's gone. He just doesn't understand. You often write in words like: "Willingly," "hopefully," "ruefully," "innocuously," just to help indicate the pace, to stop the actor a bit.

At first, as I said, it was instinct. Then you begin to learn from each person you work with. I've learned from so many. My husband, Jay, was originally a stand-up black-face comedian. He was Al Jolson's understudy when he started out in show business. Jay was always full of jokes and switches. Just unconsciously, I absorbed a great deal from him.

And, I think that, with each show and each script that you write, you learn from your*self*. And I firmly believe that some probing into yourself—even if not through analysis—is vital if you're going to be a comedy writer, because if you don't know where you're at, you don't know where the laughs are.

F: When did you first become conscious of various techniques?

RF: It was in one of the first lessons Crews taught us at Northwestern.

F: Would you say that you had this capacity instinctively and that in class, this native instinct became formalized for you.

RF: Yes. Professor Crews gave certain writing instructions which I still believe are basic. For instance: Never stare at a blank page. However bad it is, write something. As long as you've got something on the page, there is something to work with. Subconsciously you may write something that could trigger you off into a marvelous thing. You might write thirty pages and only use two of them. But that may be necessary, to clear your mind, to help you know exactly where you are.

Also, you should work from the top down to the bottom, switching the characters if you need to. Maybe the wrong people are saying the lines. Maybe you're playing it too heavy, try it for laughs instead. Take out all the straight lines.

It could be that a joke is hanging you up. A very funny joke. However funny it is, if it is stopping your scene, get it the hell out of there! By the same token, never be ashamed of an old joke. If it fits, it belongs. However old it may be, it's always new to somebody. That little girl out there will laugh at: "Did you take a bath Saturday night?" "No, why? Is there one missing?" It's the oldest joke in the Business, but she hasn't heard it before.

And you've got to believe in your material, just as actors must be able to believe a joke before they can tell it. If they don't believe it, they can't tell it.

Another thing. Don't fight the actor. If he can't say the line, find a better one for him. As long as he can't say it, he's never going to get it across to the audience.

Then there is one other basic rule. In a comedy script, *every single line* should either further the plot, develop a character, or get a laugh. If it doesn't do any of these three things—or hopefully all of them—it should go. That's a great guiding principle because in comedy you have to get right down to the bare essentials. You don't have time to fool around.

Another secret is letting the audience know something the people on the screen don't know. That pleases the audience; it gives them a moderate feeling of superiority. It's particularly good if what is happening on the screen is something that has happened to them. That provides a catharsis; and it's great therapy. I guess comedy really is a way of releasing your hostilities . . . , at least some of it plays that role, but very comfortably.

F: By the way, typically, what sort of relationship do you establish with the comedians, the actors and actresses who'll be saying your lines?

RF: Mostly, I've been typecast to work with women, lady stars. My relationship has always been pretty good with women. And, of course, supporting the stars are all the character comedians. If you've got any sense as a writer, you make friends with them right off the bat. You do this because, in many cases, the star of the show will not be as good as your character comedians. These people are giants and you hope they'll be cast in your show. If you know they are, you give them everything you can, because they're going to make the star look good. The trick is to avoid making the star feel that she isn't getting the laughs, to give her the feeling that she is promoting or facilitating them. The stars may get very nervous if they don't have all the jokes—despite the fact that the greatest example of this, Jack Benny, never did the joke himself. He reacted; he let all the people around him have the punchline.

As far as close relationships go, I should also mention that nowadays the free-lance writer just doesn't *get* too close to the show. They're not around during the shooting because they're already busy working on another script. I think that contributes to a great many writers getting cavalier about scripts. They know that chances are the story editor is going to rewrite them or that they'll be changed on the set, and this produces a certain disenchantment.

Another terrible thing that goes on today, which means that there is really no point in fighting in a story conference over whether something is funny or not is that they can easily state it's *going* to be funny—because they are going to push the laugh machine.

We're breeding a whole set of people holding the reins, who never worked with an audience in their lives. They simply don't know what it *means* to work with an audience. The guy comes in with the machine and he plays it like a piano. As he does it, the producer says, "No, wait a minute, I want a smaller laugh," or "I want a bigger laugh," or "Can we get a rollback?" "Give us a rollback." A rollback is where somebody starts to laugh and then the whole audience gets to laughing.

Another thing in freelancing is that when they ask you to make changes, you'll make them if you're smart. They've got the ultimatum; the cliché of all times: "Either you make the changes or *we'll* make them." To protect the script and yourself, you make the changes, however much you don't agree. From a practical point of view, you could lose credit if someone else makes the changes, and, if you lose credit, you're losing half of your residuals.

It's Robert Ruark's line—not mine—"What do you do for a living?" "I take in writing." If you're doing a show freelance, you *are* taking in writing and you should always keep that in mind. You can't get temperamental about it.

F: I detect from what you're saying that you prefer to have the closer relationship with your customers.

RF: Yes, I do. I like being part of the scene very much; I really enjoy that. But, I also like working to order, on demand.

A: What aspect of that?

RF: Maybe it's the challenge; or maybe it could be that, having been successful at it, I feel comfortable in it. Marlo Thomas has a marvelous way of getting you to change a line. She'll say: "Oh, this is *so* funny. Couldn't we make it funnier?" Everyone is right out there on the set, waiting. So it's a challenge—"Can I do it?" Sometimes they're so grateful to have you change the line at all that they'll accept a line that isn't half as good. Maybe they were uncomfortable about the original one. Anyway, it makes a lot of difference to them that you made the effort.

Oh, I forgot a way of handling the producers' changes when they want you to insert some provocative lines. Put a *real* dirty joke in, or a very dirty word, or something horrible. They get so uptight with that; they say: "You *can't* say that," and you say, "Aw, why not?" and give them a little trouble about it. Finally you agree to leave it out, and then they won't bug you about the thing you wanted all along!

A: Do you have a favorite chair, or notebook, or any special props you've used in getting down to write through the years?

RF: No, mainly because of working at studios . . . I don't have time for that kind of nonsense. First of all, the studio accomodations aren't that fancy. When we were at Warner Brothers, they had a big fence behind the Writer's Building. The joke was that two writers got over the fence and halfway up the hill before the machine guns got them.

When I was with MGM, bluejays started to come around, and I began to feed them. They eventually would fly right into the office and sit on the desk, on the type-writer. The next year the female birds brought their babies—just like *Born Free*. Joe Pasternak was my producer then and he would go out of his mind. He'd say, "Get those fucking birds out of here."

But I work in terrific disorder. It just gets messier and messier. No room for props. All I need is about eight pots of coffee and three or four cigarettes going at once. I could quit anything except smoking. It's such a vital part of me. I find that I can cut down on smoking when I'm not working, but the minute I start to work . . . it's part of the whole thing. I *do* like a good, black typewriter tape —where the print comes up good and sharp. That's mar-velous; it gets you going. If you're bogged down and can't do a thing, change your ribbon. It's like starting fresh. That's part of the ritual, you see, all the ways of keeping you *away* from the typewriter. You have to have another cup of coffee; there's a story conference in ten minutes; you've got to make some phone calls, or order some groceries. Changing the typewriter ribbon is marvelous, because I spend a good half hour on it, not only changing it, but getting all the ink off my fingers, getting my nails clean. And when you sit down, it's nice and black.

I had a brilliant idea once that didn't work. There's a special typewriter that types like print. I thought: Boy, I'm going to get one of those, because when the script comes to them and it looks like print, they won't *dare* change it. There's something about print that people respect. But, no sir, not a bit. They didn't respect it one bit! They changed the lines just as much.

I find now, working at home since Jay died, that there is always a loneliness when I write, which is really dreadful. Just like when I was a kid in high school, I've begun doing my homework to the radio. Or I turn on the television set with the sound off, just to be able to look up and see the people is helpful.

Writing a script is very much like having a baby —the labor pains are really terrible. Then you have the baby and they take it away from you and you're not allowed to see it. You don't know who's got it, or what they've named it or what they're going to do with it, and you feel kind of abandoned. *But,* it *isn't* your baby; you have to keep reminding yourself; it isn't really yours. *And* I've become pretty well-disciplined. I really can't let go until the job's done. I can make myself say, "All right, that's enough for today," and walk away from it, but I can't walk away from it in my head. I dream about it, too. I dream marvelous solutions where the whole thing is worked out and it's great!

F: Suppose you have something that they're going to be shooting in the morning and you've got to get the script done tonight. How do you go about this?

RF: Like I said before, you just *do* it. You don't wait for the light bulb to come on. At one point, I began to keep a notebook by the side of my bed. I would wake up and write down my "dream solution." And, in the morning, it was totally illegible!

A famous story concerns George Wells who was working for Joe Pasternak at the time. Joe was always enthralled with writers; he loved them; thought that there was a real mystique about them. He asked George: "How do you get your ideas?" and George said, "I don't know; sometimes I get them in the shower." Later that day they were working on a tough scene and they couldn't find a solution to it. The next morning they met outside the stage as they were coming to work and Joe said, "Did you think of a solution?" George said, "Not yet." And Joe answered, "Why? Didn't you take a shower?"

But I don't just work on material in my sleep. I also do it in the daytime. Maybe I'm driving along in the car, and I begin acting out the scene. I come to a stoplight. I'm saying, "No, I will NOT, and furthermore . . ." I look up and there's somebody staring at me, and quickly I make like I'm *singing!*

Sometimes, I'll use a tape-recorder in the car for whatever occurs to me. Or, if I think I'm in a creative state where I might get ideas and not remember them, I'll keep the recorder with me, even put it by the bed when I go to sleep.

A: You use the recorder quite a bit?

RF: Oh, yes. Particularly, because in story conferences, as I mentioned, you may hit on an idea that pleases you all and start to laugh at it. And you might laugh at it so much that you forget what it was.

I wish I had touch with some of the earliest ideas . . . Mother found something I wrote when I was six years old, when I was making lots of things up. As a matter of fact, she tells me that when I was very young, my grandmother got extremely upset because I would lie on the couch staring up at the ceiling. They'd all get very nervous about that and say, "What are you doing?" I'd say: "I'm making up my dreams," and my grandmother would say "You've got to stop her," because she thought I was nuts.

In fact, until eighth grade, I had a tough time with English, because my writing was spoken, written to be spoken, and I had to learn to do it differently. But that year I had a teacher, a marvelous teacher who said to me: "I think that you are going to go to Hollywood and become a scenario writer. You must keep on doing this because you write writing to be spoken and not to be read." It wasn't until years later that I remembered her saying this, because, at the time, it seemed like such a ridiculous notion.

I certainly wasn't trying to be a writer at that time. All I knew was that no matter what I did, I couldn't get an "A"!!

Summary

So, Ruth Flippen entered show biz via "My Man."

Certainly, a three-year-old is unaware of the full meaning of such a song of pathos, of sexuality, and of human loss. But the adults of that Depression era knew, as Ruth's parents must have known, that in an audience already worn down with the burden of financial struggle or loss, this kind of song was a particularly effective one.

And little Ruth became "Baby Ruth" on that unforgettable poster so reminiscent of the Depression *zeitgeist:*

"Baby Ruth Tonight! Free Spaghetti!"

When one tries to picture her family life, that household sheltering three generations and the unwanted ghost of poverty, one sees it as widely typical, save for the presence of the little child star. It is as though the parents had coaxed Ruth to get up on that stage so that they might, in some way, be different from every other average family of the times. This is one of the pictures we get from Ruth herself, who was and is aware of herself as a "princess" with a little kingdom of subjects.

This is not to say that she played this crucial and nuclear role in her family without conflict. On the contrary, she describes that her parents fought frequently over the appropriateness of her position. Her father, as she told us, was always trying to "filter her down," yet he seems to have been less effective than her mother who clearly facilitated Ruth's career, molded her, and then lived vicariously through her.

Ruth's description of how she learned her original routines is of special interest. Learning theory advocates could point it out as excellent subjective evidence for their theories. Ruth tells us that she thinks she "was more like a chimpanzee, imitating, and learning how to do cute things."

Why did she do this? For the social reinforcement. Witness that quintessential paragraph that could describe any very young show-biz or performing child:

"You're put up there on the stage; you're taught that approval is important; at first, you don't know how or why you're getting it, but you know somehow that it's part of the love and approval you need to get from your parents. And, you know, it's kind of awful when you *don't* get a hand, or when people laugh at you and you don't even know why."

Here was a child like most children, needing the reinforcement of others (very *externally*-oriented at this point), trying to get a handle on how to go through the routines that bring her what she wants, and gradually eliminating what she does not. She went along with the direction given her by her mother, although in the later days she hates seeing herself in that light, "I was very precocious, and really just a horrible child. I wouldn't *have* a child like that in my own home!"

Ruth describes the search to "get a handle on what will get you another hand." For her this is an explanation of how the comic senses develop, "You're either going to get a laugh or you're going to cry a lot." And joking became then, even at a very young age, onstage and off, a major means of getting what she needed. Along the way, even by the time she was six, she had a "knack" for choosing the right song for the right audience.

It is interesting that, in looking back, Ruth indicates that she didn't really feel she had a very good voice, or that she was particularly talented as a dancer. One wonders how she thought she measured up. She seems to have shown a lot of confidence and self-esteem when she was a child, giving her the courage to confront adults. It also seems that she had the greatest *chutzpah* where she had the greatest success and rewards—with adults. It seems likely that she thought of herself as being pretty good, or she wouldn't have been able to pull off her act with such success.

A key to the underlying ambivalent nature of Ruth's situation is her appearing at the age of eight on a bill following a stripper. Ruth is still affected by this, saying, "They really didn't care *how* they exposed kids then."

Added to the inappropriateness of many routines Ruth went through was the fact that she sometimes "bombed"; and that was for her a terrible experience. She doesn't dwell on this, but it no doubt affected her and might have contributed to the fact that, in later years, performing was not her chosen way of life. She also mentions feeling the isolation, the discrimination and even scorn associated with being in show business. It hurt her peer relationships and, despite her success, left her with the "hang-up" that "because I was in show business, I was slightly less than everyone else."

These factors apparently contributed to Ruth's obvious happiness with the success achieved in college where, although she continued in the arts, she was writing and achieving academically.

The pattern of her early life, however, led to a life-style which did remain with Ruth. She has gravitated toward people older than herself, just as she did when, as a child, she did what was necessary to obtain the positive reinforcement. Through high school, she lived a life different from her peers; she felt apart from her age group, and so stuck with adults. She went so far as to marry a man "a great deal older than I." In many ways, as she says, "I looked on Jay as a father." (He was J. C. Flippen, the late, fine character actor).

Ruth clearly realizes the effect upon her life of her mother's having "natural talents that weren't developed."

Her mother even had to try out writing and Ruth found it necessary to stress to her mother, just after the tragic death of her husband, that "we are not going to be the Dolly Sisters any more." Her mother, it is clear, was a true victim of environment control, wanting "to be a part of it—the fans, the autographs, the limelight . . . she kind of wishes I had kept my original path and become a star." The strength of her mother's relationship with her, combined with a blossoming independence and sense of personal achievement contributed to Ruth's expanding into a craft with which her mother was unfamiliar and uncomfortable. Ruth was becoming her own person.

As did other writers in this study, Ruth went through the Depression years, and used humor "as a natural defense." She tried to fight off the domestic struggles and the sound and impact of them with joking. Ruth realizes that, although this can be an asset, it can also be a liability, a wobbly crutch if used inappropriately. For the show-biz kid, in particular, the reinforcement received for being a star and using comedy successfully on the stage can be such a powerful influence that it may be difficult to control it offstage. Ruth indicates that she does not like the *defensive* aspect of humor in her life, and consciously tries to prevent herself from "going for the laugh every time."

The story conference is an experience where, as a woman, she has to "be kind of careful not to hurt masculine feelings and pride." At these moments, Ruth may be lured by the pull of power and former experiences of external reinforcement. But now, her greatest source of satisfaction is from within. Also, she realizes she may blow her ideas and their significance, and her dignity as a human being, by acting things out all the time. Even though she understands the technical aspects of humor creation, many of which she learned in school, she knows this is still a struggle for her. Herein, she can still be involved in measuring out for herself which value is primary—internal dignity, or external recognition.

Ruth indicates how "degrading" it feels when she is involved with trying to please everyone. Soon she begins to feel used, "like a whore must feel." This seems to bring her back to memories of her childhood, when she was angry (without knowing it) at the adults for putting her in the position of playing out all those absurd routines.

There can't be a better description of the pull between external and internal reinforcement, nor of the struggle of a woman to build her own strengths so that she controls her life. Sometimes, for dignity's sake, she will get a "side remark in . . . here or there." This reestablishes her uniqueness and rescues her from feeling used. Ruth eloquently describes her position in the Business —fighting for her maintenance of worth against many non-creative people.

She indicates her ability to carry through by herself by telling us that she customarily writes alone. She wants to solve the problem herself "when I take in writing"—reminiscent of descriptions of internal motivation. She considers calling up other writers or friends for advice or sharing unfinished material to be "cheating." This is the way she was taught to write (technically) in college; however, it appears that Ruth's pattern of solitary writing has deeper roots than her having been so instructed. She proves that she can make it without the applause and approval of others; she can fully test her worth by her own measures.

Psychologists trying to unite behavioristic and humanistic approaches thus view the role of self-reinforcement in human life. This characteristic may be a test of the natively creative—can she be the leader of her own program, risking the compromise of her work in deference to contingencies set down by others?

The information in this section about creativity and the process of creating is rich and of great value—but we have focused instead on these other factors in Ruth's life. We suggest, however, that the reader study her descriptions of the daily life of show business. There is exceptional detail on how decisions are made, how stories are put together, how one works strategically in getting along with others on the "team."

Ruth believes that there is a large number of techniques which can be learned, "and that writing can be like 'housework.'" No doubt this is a partial product of her early conditioning, which made it possible to figure out swiftly how to please others and turn them on. She also gives some credence to the notion that there is a native potential which contributes to being a "humor creator." Here is her most definitive statement in that regard:

> "I think that if somebody wants to be an acrobat, well, sure it helps if they're double-jointed! But, if they're not, there are ways to teach people to do a walk-over or a back-spin. You can," she says, "teach them to be limber . . . if they want to work on the exercises."

She states that she feels she "learned the professional game," and the conviction that, "If you're in that arena, it's seeping into you."

In view of the impact of Ruth's learning against the backdrop of her being originally externally-motivated, it is interesting that she abhors the "laugh machine" technology and the element of automatic response or formula in the Industry.

Ruth is still in there fighting, feeling the power of her own internal force. She fights by getting in that "side remark" here and there, and using "their" strategy to do it. She doesn't get temperamental, but works to "protect" the script and herself. She feels terrible when they take "that baby" (her script) away from her, but realizes "it isn't really hers."

Baby Ruth grown up—no longer the "horrible," manipulating child she described to us, but instead an intelligent woman able to cope with the pressures of the Industry by solving problems, putting herself out there, carefully, but steadily—being her own person within the boundaries of the large and impersonalized television industry where they can push buttons to create laughter. We feel that Ruth has provided us with a dignified and appealing portrait of a most unusual human being. In her, we see both creative and conforming aspects, and we experience, through her, our own struggle to create ourselves and remain ourselves.

Bob Henry

Laugh With, Laugh At

BOB HENRY began his career in radio as an announcer and disc jockey, eventually becoming a performer at the old Knickerbocker Music Hall. As a performer, he went for an interview with Ernie Glocksman, the then producer of the Martin and Lewis Show. "Tell me you're a stage manager," Glocksman greeted him. "I don't need a comic. Do you know how to make a production break-down?" Henry told him yes, although he didn't know. The Secretary showed him what a production breakdown was: scenery, props, wardrobe. "We had no desk," he wrote, "I worked off the ledge of a window. That was my start in television."

Since then Bob Henry has written, directed, and produced for Nat King Cole, Gisele McKenzie, Dinah Shore, Carl Reiner, George Gobel, Andy Williams, Lena Horne, Jose Feliciano, and Perry Como. More currently he has written for Flip Wilson and Gladys Knight and the Pips.

The sour wine of hostility is usually drunk from two bowls. One bowl carries the label "worthlessness and inferiority." The other bowl is "vulnerability." They are interchangeable; most angry persons have quaffed from both. Violence is the virulent "mariage" which results when hostility and aggression are blended. The pestilence caused by exposure to this concoction is long-lived, widespread, and frequently lethal.

For centuries, mankind has contemplated its mirror and agonized on issues relating to these elements of human behavior. The biblical story of Cain and Abel reflects this tortured preoccupation and describes the consequences of violence, "And now art thou cursed from the earth . . . When thou tillest the ground, it shall not . . . yield unto thee her strength; a fugitive and a vegetable shalt thou be in the earth." And Cain lamented his fate, "my punishment is greater than I can bear."

On occasions, a lack of precision in definition increases the controversy over violence, hostility, and aggression. In this book we use the word "aggression" in a most general sense—as that inherent biologic force which gives impetus to all behavior. Thus, it refers to *all* forceful and active behavior. In this sense, aggression is a valued element, even essential to the functioning of living creatures. The degree of torpor that would exist without this force is difficult to comprehend. Perhaps any life beyond the vegetative level would be impossible.

In many ways, the professional writers in this book illustrate the positive power of aggression. An aggressive urge stimulated Bob Henry, the subject of this specific interview, to try telling jokes one summer night at the

Boston ballroom where his band was playing, with the weather too hot for dancing. Aggression stimulated him to seek ever better jobs, from Boston to Cape Cod, from Providence to Boston again, to Stamford, to New York City. Aggression sent him to win the Old Knickerbocker Music Hall amateur contest. Aggression was the vital force catalyzing so many of his stunning successes.

By our definition we mean to isolate that special category of aggression where forcefulness creates destruction. This category we identify as "violence," with hostility as the dominant emotion. Violence is an archaic reflex, a relic from simpler existences of more bestial creatures. It is, essentially, a simplistic attempt to bulldoze an "easy way" solution in complex experiences which, by their very nature, demand at least some degree of intelligent thought for satisfactory resolution. It is clear from many considerations that violence is the true pornography.

Violence is widely condemned, but widely practiced. There are many forms of violence: "semi-official violence" and "personal violence," mental or psychological violence covert violence. "Semi-official violence" includes outrages committed against the natural biosphere—extinction of animal and vegetable species, ravage of finite natural resources, exploitation of the land and sea and atmosphere. "Personal violence" includes all acts of physical and mental brutality.

It is clear that violence is more than physical offense with its obvious physical trauma. There is much mental violence committed in the world, with disastrous consequences to both victim and perpetrator. To psychiatrist Fredric Wertham, a most dreadful consequence of violence is its dehumanizing effects on both victim and perpetrator. This dehumanization derives in part from disrespect for human rights and the sanctity of each person's existence—a disrespect that marks each violent act. By violence, all humans are debased. The presence of any form of violence—physical or mental, private or political, overt or hidden—scorns belief that mankind has emerged to any degree from the ancient fogs of bloodlust and cannabalism.

The reasons for man's aggressive force to take these destructive bents are still unclear. Some authorities, such as psychiatrist Albert Rothenberg, blame heredity. Others report that violence breeds violence, by the influence of family example. Behavioral scientists Larry Silver, Christina Dublin, and Reginald Lourie concluded from their studies, "The child who experiences violence as a child has the potential of becoming a violent member of society in the future."

Many people express the criticism that, among environmental forces stimulating tendencies toward violence, the various entertainment media down through the ages have contributed their share. It is argued that through these media violence is made more widely familiar and a tolerance is developed. Distress is expressed that social sanction for violence is implied in widespread presentation through the channels of public recreation. Although themes of violence can be recognized in entertainment items throughout history, modern television violence raises the greatest concern because of the very large worldwide audiences exposed to its example.

It would be very appropriate to ask what place a discussion on violence has in a book on humor. There can be no question about all humor being *aggressive*. It is so, if only by definition: it is active, creative, instructive, an assault upon the *status quo*. It is all of these, even when its aggressiveness is not joined by hostility to commit a violence against some person(s). Except in the eyes of a limited few, this aggressive essence is no condemnation of humor.

However, everyone interested in humor must come, at some time or other, to the agonizing realization that even this sweetness, this touchstone, this elixir may be used in the service of violence. In fact, there are some whose experiences with humor have been so unfortunate and so one-sidedly limited that they identify humor as violence. This association of humor with violence is especially shocking when its powerful capacities for enlightenment, mind expansion, stimulation of creativeness become potent agents for destruction and annihilation. Also distastefully ironic is the fact that humor—such a valuable catalyst in bringing people together for shared pleasure—may be used in such ways that drive people apart and destroy the fabric of their communion.

In this interview, Bob Henry in many ways demonstrates his sensitivity to the potentials for violence in humor. His professional work is signatured by this same indication of compassionate concern. Bob Henry's childhood distress over psychological violence is documented in his comments, "My mother had to go to work when she was growing up . . . She had a drive my father never had . . . She pushed everyone. Her push was like a shout —gently given, without love. She would push my brother . . . She often put my brother down, too. And I'd die, I'd say, 'Mom, that's no way to talk to any human being.'" Even at that young age Bob was beginning to be able to make sharp differentiation between general aggressiveness and specific violence.

Most classifications of humor list the categories "hostile humor"—in which someone's distress is the objective of the humor—and "superiority humor"—in which an objective is the establishment of superiority of one person or group over another. Important research on these forms of humor has been carried out by various scientists, including psychologists Donald Byrne, Walter O'Connell, and Patricia and Donald Spiegel. Psychiatrist Lawrence Kubie commented, "The critical difference is between smiling or laughing *with* someone or smiling and laughing *at* them."

Bob Henry documents in this interview his knowledge of and wisdom about hostility humor and superiority humor. Specific examples will be cited in our summary remarks following his interview. Many humorists and humor enthusiasts prefer to ignore these forms of humor. Bob Henry has courageously faced the issues raised by them; he has undoubtedly given much deliberate thought to the subject.

We take in this discussion an example from his informed concern. His example has inspired a deeper inquiry into the subject than is usually our inclination in matters of violence. Expressed above is our general impression that violence is the true pornography. But, we find that violence in humor is a more complex story.

We respect the unhappy sentiments and wounded feelings of the many who have suffered as objects of ridicule, mockery, sarcasm, witticism, caricature, teasing, and other forms of hostile humor. And, we are not interested in going down in history as hypocritical apologists for the hostile components and manifestations of humor. But other factors must be considered.

A hint of the presence of these other factors can be found in a comment by the famous comedian Jack E. Leonard. "An insult is only funny when it's ridiculous, and it's ridiculous if it's aimed at some really big shot."

Many scientific studies—including some by one of the authors (Fry) with psychologist Lawrence Pinneo—suggest a very significant, basic evolutionary role in human *survival* for those experiences associated with smiling and laughter. In shedding light on this survival role, perspective calls for modification of the view that all hostile humor is all bad. Paradoxically—in view of the poisonous words and tendencies of some humor—a certain part of the smiling and laughter associated with that kind of humor is engaged, on the instinctual or unconscious level, in the stimulation of appeasement and the inhibition of physical violence. Behavioral scientists point out the large number of appeasement or inhibitory signals put out by all animals—including man. There can be little doubt that were it not for humor—even hostile humor—considerable more physical violence between humans would occur. Here, we have one form of violence actually *inhibiting*, not merely substituting for another form of violence.

A step beyond such basic considerations is the role that the quality of empathy plays. Empathy might be called that emotive-intellectual state which results when one person is able to understand how another might feel or perceive a given situation. Put more simply: you put yourself into the shoes of another. Empathy diminishes any tendency toward violence.

Humor enhances the development of empathy in two ways. One is on the side of the knowledge-expanding effect of humor. Through the magic of the punchline, humor gives each participant a bit of knowledge of which he had not been aware prior to delivery of the punchline. These are wisdom pills with sugar coating. The wisdom gives us the ability to broaden our view of others, in that most humor is about experiences and themes common to all human life. Even the most derogatory ethnic humor contains some tiny elements of this perspective-broadening potential. Even when humor is used in a vicious manner, the humorist must receive some information about ways in which he and his victim are in the same boat of human existence.

A second aspect of the empathy-enhancing quality of all humor is its characteristic of being a shared experience. The sharing of a joke, even at one's own expense, is a joint participation emphasizing the mutual humanness of the participants. Certainly Bob Henry's early experience when his band was playing a gig in Boston, on that fateful summer night too hot to dance, is a good example of shared participation. He began to tell a few jokes and ended up wondering in a humorous style whether he was a joke-telling musician or a saxophone-playing comedian.

We want to be explicit about our reservations on this specific subject. Yes, there is the tendency in humor to enhance empathy—this tendency is much more developed when hostility is not part of the mirth. Certainly, we need to recognize that tendency, but we also realize that its presence only modulates the undesirability of hostile humor; it does not eliminate it. Further, there are other, better ways to stimulate empathy than hostile humor—perhaps none better than that sweet humor which is truly shared mirth.

Another factor to be considered in our judgment of hostile humor has to do with the abstract nature of humor. Humor may be utilized in the service of hostility; but it does not draw blood. Wit may be "as sharp as a rapier"; teasing may be "as pointed as a needle." But wit is neither rapier, nor is teasing made of steel. Hostile humor is not lethal. It is already one huge step away from the sword, the firebrand, the club or gun. One *lives* with humor, "to fight again." Its abstract nature, though it may be violent in content or intent, spares life and therefore does not destroy hope.

Taking this issue a step further, we find hostile humor actually having the potentiality of being a substitute for physical violence. This value has been the especial interest of anthropologists, psychologists, and other behavioral scientists, including Jacob Levine, Rose Coser, Pamela Bradney, Donald Hayworth, Jacqueline Goodchilds, and Ewart Smith. Psychologists Anne Goodrich, Jules Henry, and Wells Goodrich stated, "Laughter is an important and acceptable way in which a group can participate in and enjoy the disparagement of others . . . group laughter functions as a mechanism for promoting solidarity and providing a safety valve for divisive tensions."

As a substitute for direct physical violence, hostile humor avoids bloody destruction, and can intensify the solidarity of a group structure. It is clear that substitution benefit is greatest in the group context. An individual committing mental or emotional violence as a separate, lonely act will suffer the emotional consequences of his act—guilt, depression, etc.—as he would if the act were physical—perhaps less strongly, but suffer he will. This suffering is apparently moderated when his humor functions for some group objective, furthers a group goal. The individual is then supported by group approbation and is gratified by the good he has contributed to the group. For the group, itself, this substitution of hostile humor for physical violence is directly beneficial for the survival of the group, both from the standpoint of maintaining its numeric size and from that of maintaining a general conformity to survival values and behavior.

An additional factor to be considered as mitigating the negative status of hostile humor is the cathartic function of mirth. As we have discussed in an earlier chapter, the Freudian concept of humor describes build-up of affect—anxiety, anger, sexual tension, etc.—which is sud-

denly reduced in cathartic relief with the precipitation of
mirth. Jacob Levine summarized this theory, "Humorous
stimuli are gratifying because prohibited wishes operating
largely as psychological forces originating in the unconscious are momentarily permitted release. The anxiety
which normally accompanies the expression of these impulses is reduced." Martin Grotjahn said, "Jokes grow
best on the graves of old anxieties . . . Wit gives freedom,
and laughter is the expression of such freedom."

We have stated that humor involves more than
tension-relief. However, to the extent that catharsis does
take place, hostile humor will serve to drain built-up
stores of hostility which otherwise could eventuate in
other more undesirable kinds of violence. It is easy to
recognize how this catharsis benefits the morale and
equilibrium of individuals. It is clear that benefit is to be
found in group settings as well.

The role of the clown or jester or fool sheds light on
the process of group catharsis. Sociologists Arlene and
Richard Daniels commented on the social function of the
"career fool," (who acts the fool in any group), "Fools help
define the range and level of group performance . . . One
can expect the formation of (fool) roles as the precipitates
of social interaction in which clashing interests may themselves be stabilized through the (fools)." And Jacob
Levine, exploring the significance of the clown in American Indian tribes, stated, "His permissive clowning . . .
(vicariously gratifies) all the forbidden fantasies and instinctual strivings of the group, without fear of reprisal. By
the gaiety and laughter he evokes in the group, he provides a catharsis for its deepest and most basic antisocial
feelings."

Slapstick comedy, found in most cultures in most
historic eras, represents an extension of the clown role
in catharsis of hostility. Axiomatically, slapstick is
the acting-out of violence, but within the sheltering
framework of playful comedy, with the result that violent
tendencies are acted upon and no harm is done. The
specific action of slapstick in cultural catharsis has not
been studied so intensively as that of the clown or fool.

However, historical perspective brings forth the discovery that slapstick enjoys its greatest public enthuasiasm at times when a society is undergoing strife and challenge. The challenge has commonly been that of integrating different population groups together, or different value orientations. The strife has commonly been difficulties of economic hardship or territorial conflict. Examples illustrating this timing include the phallic slapstick of pre-classic Greece, commedia dell'arte of post-Renaissance Europe, minstrel shows of post-Civil War, and the vaudeville and movie slapstick of the western world during the Great Depression. Slapstick has enjoyed a recent revival, mostly in the movies, but also somewhat on television. This increased popularity may be a reflection of contemporary troubled times.

Knowledge and research about the cathartic role of hostile humor leads us to believe that it makes a palpable contribution, on both the individual and group levels, to mitigate the various and many horrors resulting in human circles from class conflicts, racial discrimination, sexual exploration, economic imbalance. Not a devitalizing opiate, hostile humor provides cathartic relief from the weakening and paralyzing effects of frustration and indignation. It thus contributes to development of more creative, more productive solutions to individual and cultural problems by making possible more careful, less tumultuous cerebration.

One further factor indicates the complexity of judgment on hostile humor. This factor has to do with humor's general role as one of mankind's most commonly used and most universally accepted coping mechanisms. In all the ways we discuss here, and in others either unknown to us or less germaine to the thrust of this book, humor serves to grapple with the problems of living and dying that challenge man's existence.

As with any other tool, or coping mechanism, we may use it inappropriately, awkwardly, destructively. None of us is perfect and each is liable to the errors and mistakes which humility leads us to expect and forgive, and from which arrogance is no protection.

Our flawed use of humor can be no condemnation of humor itself, but rather of the manner of the usage. And, in addition, humor—even when at its worst, in hostile humor—stands out from most other coping mechanisms used by humans, in that it always has its mind-expanding, creative element. With the sword, with the insult, with swearing, with hateful reviling, no one learns anything that does him much good. With even violent humor, one *may not* learn anything valuable or informative, but that possibility *is* inherent in the humor.

Konrad Lorenz wrote in *On Aggression*, "Humor and knowledge are the two great hopes of civilization."

Interview

Fry: How did you get into the humor business?

Henry: I was blessed or cursed with a comedic talent. Recently, while doing the Flip Wilson show, I felt especially "blessed." I had originally thought of going to medical school, but in my second year—while taking qualitative analysis—I knew I wasn't the scientific type who becomes a good doctor. Oh, I had a great bedside manner; I could have been a warm doctor, and maybe been of some therapeutic value that way. But it was an uphill push so far as physics and chemistry and biology went. My last try at it was in my junior year, and then I addressed myself to a theatrical focus.

I played saxophone in a dance band in Boston—my home town. I was the Master of Ceremonies who led the dance games, you know, the kind where you throw one shoe out and if the boy got the shoe, he'd get to dance with the girl. One night it was too hot for all that. I tried out some jokes I remembered from the movies and the people laughed! Partly they laughed because I was funny, but mostly because they were bored. It was amazing to me. I got so encouraged. I would say after that: "I don't know whether I'm a musician who tells jokes or a comedian who plays an instrument." Before long, I was putting on a show every Saturday night. It was very akin to the Borscht circuit shows in the New York Catskills. I would write a sketch or recreate skits I'd seen in burlesque or musical shows in Boston. I always had a great memory for those. I recreated them; I wrote them and I performed them.

That kind of thing had really started at home when I was younger. I'd recreate movies in the kitchen for my family. My father would sit at the head of the table and I'd do everyone, the Marx Brothers, Charlie Chaplin, everyone. They laughed, but I never thought anything about it at the time because I come from a family who liked show business.

My father was a barber and my mother was the head of a domestic employment agency, but I was brought up exposed to the theater. They loved the theater. I saw, "The Big Parade," I was six years old then; I saw the original "No, No, Nanette" sitting behind a post in the second balcony. The other kids would play baseball on Saturday afternoons while I sat in the Shubert Theater for 55¢, up there in the balcony. No kid could understand that.

We were doing these things for fun, but they worked their way into my system and I developed this real feeling for pantomime. While I was in college, I performed in a summer camp. I became the hit of the season. And after I graduated, in 1940, I felt I should pursue a theatrical career.

Allen: Did you always have good reactions to your performing?

H: Well, yes, except in certain night-clubs in Boston where I could hear my diction being too good. I'd come out and say, "Good evening, ladies and gentlemen," and I'd feel truck drivers looking up from their beers and thinking, "Where'd this guy come from?" I was generally too smart for the room except where the room was smart. Most of the big comedians then, the Bob Hopes, the Red Skeltons, weren't college graduates. Today, I'm happy to say that they run toward Woody Allen more. He may not be a college graduate but he's a most literate man. Flip, too, even though he never went beyond the eighth grade. He's got his own "degree."

Anyway, how did I become a comedian? I decided I wasn't a night-club comic. My material was too clean. I decided that I was more suitable for radio. So in order to work my way into radio entertainment, I thought I'd start from the bottom up. I took classes at Emerson College one night a week on how to be a radio announcer. I got a job at a small station on Cape Cod where I did everything from sweeping the floors to interviewing Gertrude Lawrence, who was there on tour. I was paid $20 a week and I was very lucky, in truth, to get it.

From Cape Cod, I graduated to Providence, R.I. But luck wasn't so good there and I subsequently went back to Boston. I got a radio job and met the girl who later became my wife. She was secretary to the treasurer; her name was on my pay check every week.

I "rose" to disc jockey and was making $35 a week. That sounds ridiculous today, but then it was the going rate. As the "afternoon man," I had to make jokes between the records. I was popular with the kids because I knew the music, Benny Goodman, Artie Shaw, whoever, and I could name whoever was playing the solos at a given moment. Before I realized it, I started getting stacks of mail, fan mail, which my wife would answer for me. It finally penetrated that I was too—that I had outgrown Boston. I went to Matt Kelly at NBC in New York to get a job. I said, "I'm 4-F." He said "Everybody is 4-F." I went to another station and said, "I'm a big-shot in Boston." They had big shots from all over and the guy who interviewed me spelled that out to me.

I ended up in Stamford, Connecticut, but made regular trips into New York, where I finally got a job in FM. I wrote script material for classical music shows; I did biographies; all sorts of things like that. I won an amateur contest at a place called the Old Knickerbocker Music Hall and won a week's engagement there but stayed the whole season. I was highbrow at the purely classical music station and I'd don makeup at night and do my comedy routine at the Music Hall. I was right for that room. It was camp, old-time, sawdust on the floor, red and white tablecloths, and I was perfect. Many of the people I worked with made it later. Jack Lemmon was one of them; Gene Barry, Jack Allison, Juanita Hall were others. I learned a lot because I was out there six nights a week, two shows a night. This was at the end of the war, in '46 and '47.

A: Were you writing your own stuff then?

H: Yes, I couldn't afford writers and I found out that I could do better than writers who came to me with their own material. There's still a lot of poor quality in comedy writing today.

A: Did you like writing?

H: Well, yes, but like many comedy writers, I procrastinated a lot between projects. I told my wife often that I'd have to generate new material or get out of the business. She was great support, had tremendous confidence, told me again and again, "you can do it, you're good at it." I also worked on this blocking with my analyst who was convinced that when my analysis came to conclusion I'd be free of the block. I went for nine years, three sessions a week.

I liked performing all the time, but writing my own stuff was a chore. The same thing still happens today. It's sitting down and getting started that's the problem. Once I'm on my way, it goes really great, there's no problem.

Anyway, around the end of the war, I began getting around to wherever people were stationed, entertaining and breaking in new material—Ellis Island, and I entertained for free at the American Theater Wing in New York. As an MC, I was very popular. The guys loved my stuff, so I got the opportunity to go to Japan to entertain troops. I felt I needed a change from radio which was going nowhere and I went overseas for nine months when the Korean War broke out. I was great for the Armed Forces, I played everywhere. The guys and the chaplains loved me because my material was funny, but clean. Cheaper comics had to resort to dirty material to get good laughs. I got good laughs with clean material. I could even do it for the Japanese. It was a great thrill when I did my monologue. I would do, for instance, an imitation of a symphonic announcer like Milton Cross: "Good evening, lovers of music, and those of you who work."

I even got so that I could work with a translator for Japanese audiences. It was a strange feeling. I'd use psychology to try to figure out what would go over with non-Americans, and what would turn them off. Often I was successful with some of the same material that bombed in Boston. The Japanese have much further depth than we—92% literacy. Also, I'm not a big guy, so I was no threat to them. I ended up knowing I could make it as a performer, but I didn't want to. It involved too much travel. I wanted to stay with my family, with my daughter who was then four. So I luckily got a production job at NBC, as a producer on the Dean Martin-Jerry Lewis Show.

An old friend of mine got me the job. He recommended me to the head producer of the show who said, "Don't tell me you're a performer. Tell me you're a stage manager, because I'm not looking for a comic." I never even had an interview. I went directly into the rehearsal hall in New York City, and Dean Martin was sitting with a blonde in one corner and Jerry Lewis was screaming out dirty songs with the pianist, while Mr. Glocksman, the producer, was saying, "Now, Jerry, now, Dean, Jerry!" He turned to me, said, "Do you know how to make a production breakdown?" I said, "Uh. . ." He said, "Good, the props are in my office." I didn't even know what a production breakdown was. His secretary showed me—scenery, props, wardrobe. We had no desk; I worked off the ledge of a window, the producer's desk or chair. That was my start in television, or at least in the production end. I worked long and hard—just as I do now. That is one of my secrets, if I may say so, the secret to doing a hit show. Then it was up the ladder, to producer-director, and that's where I am today. To my partnership with Flip—we're co-producers.

F: You mentioned that you used to do routines as a kid at home. We are wondering what sort of a role humor played in your family life.

H: With that question, Doctor, you could retire. I took my Liberal Arts degree in psychology and maybe that will help me describe those complicated dynamics to you. There aren't many of us psychologists around producing shows. I also have a lot of hours in analysis. But I'm sure there are a lot of producers with a lot of hours in analysis! Anyway, my point is I've kept my academic interest.

My mother's still alive, my father is not. There was always a great sense of humor in them, compounded by their very difficult background. My father was an immigrant from Russia, one of seven children. My mother was born in New York, one of six. When her father died, my grandmother married a tailor with seven children. Can you imagine a tailor in those days trying to support thirteen children? My mother had to go to work when she was growing up. Though, I know it sounds tough; but in those days she wasn't the only one.

My father worked as a barber six days a week, taking his dinner to work in a sack. He worked until 11 at night cutting hair. My mother worked in a beauty shop for awhile until the Depression, when that fell apart—also long and hard, only one day a week off. My father was a good barber—the top guy at Filene's Department store and later opened his own barbershop. He had a great poker face and a great sense of humor. Everything went along smoothly until the Depression and then there were personal problems between my mother and father. He was content to be a barber and she was ambitious and driving. She didn't think there was enough money, tried to make him work harder, and he couldn't. He would say, "We may have to go on welfare." To her that was scandalous. Working so hard, you just don't go on welfare. When you're one of thirteen kids and working, working, you don't go to the government for help. She had a drive my father never had. Now she's mellowed—she's in a retirement home, but not completely mellowed.

Living through this, there was a personal strain for me, for all of us. But through it all, through my mother's driving, on the back of my fairly easy-going father, there was always laughing. Father would tell jokes, often the same damn jokes again and again, and sometimes I'd laugh out of courtesy. My mother had a keen sense of humor. She could see personalities, could cut right through to the heart of what made people tick. She made a great saleslady because of her psychological techniques. She'd say, for instance when she was doing her employment agency job, "It would be a great thing for you to take this job. I think you should try it, because you'll have a great home there." She capitalized on her abilities and opened a second office, which my brother took over for awhile.

F: Did you have a special role in your family?

H: Oh boy, another very good question. Yes, I was the fair-haired child, not only because I was the younger child—my brother is six years older—but because I seemed to have a kind of sageness, or wisdom. When I was about thirteen my mother came to me and said, "Do you think we should get a new furnace with diesel oil? I said, "Coal." This was a tough decision for a kid, but she'd trust me, where she wouldn't trust my father. He was making a lot of wrong decisions so she became the dominant person. She'd often put my brother down, too. And I'd die, I'd say, "Mom, that's no way to talk to any human being." I was able to be subjective. I saw her treatment of them and pulled away from her.

Anyway, we were all blessed with humor but I seemed to have come out way ahead of the others. And it's continued to save my act in real life. Humor has been a great cushion, the major facet of my career. Most producers of comedy shows have it, Bob Finkel, Bud Yorkin, Norman Lear. You have to, you need the cushion in this business. Freud emphasized this cushion. People say he's sexy; he's not. Sex is only a mirror for what is going on. Sex is a great way to find out dynamic things about us, the society.

With our family, you could tell the difference in us by our humor. My brother was the clown, a real-life buffoon, he often came off the same in the outside world, without trying. I can turn the humor on and off.

My mother was a typical Jewish mother—she drove her children and husband. She said it was a personal affront to her when I decided to see an analyst. I can speak freely about her—I'm not damning her. I can understand her, she grew up having to make a living. She had her problems, one of thirteen kids. She didn't want us to be hungry. When she was eleven years old, she was babysitting for a child. It died in her arms. They never knew the reasons. She felt guilty; that she did wrong. That had to leave its mark somehow. And that unfortunately left a mark on us.

She pushed everyone. Her push was like a shout —gently given, without love. She would push my brother and pushed him to where he wouldn't do anything. "Don't push me, I'm not going to do anything." But me, she could not push. She tried, she wanted me to become a doctor. But I got a double F in Physics! I smiled, I cut the umbilical cord. But it cost 1200 sessions with a doctor. My mother was the problem child in my life. The delicious thing is that with her or without her, I made more money, am now making more money than she or I ever dreamed of. I am astounded. I don't know whether it's because of her or in spite of her.

F: Did anyone else in the family play a musical instrument, other than yourself.

H: My father played the fiddle, now that you mention it. We never played together. On holidays, with the fireplace going, he'd pick it up. Oh, he wasn't very good; he played simple little things. It helped as an interlude to all those driving moments that were somehow so characteristic of . . . especially of Jewish families trying to survive in that time.

F: This element of music in your life, when did you first get into music?

H: You ask me a question, I'll give you an answer. I

came out of the shower one Sunday morning and mother said, "Bob, how'd you like to play clarinet, that long black thing Ted Lewis plays?" "He has a top hat?" "Yes." I didn't think of the music, I thought of the hat. "One of my customers has a son who teaches clarinet, and I thought it would be nice—a nice Jewish boy, at least taking music lessons." I took the clarinet only as a device. I wasn't really a musician. It was a big frustration. But I like music a lot, I love listening to it, and it was a way to get on the stage, like going to radio school.

The Flip Wilson show is mostly comedy. I'm relentless in my standards for comedy writing. I'm commercial enough to recognize you can't do Shakespeare and Shaw all the time, but on my show we have three teams that write, and Herbie (Baker) in charge of them all to offset the bad times. We have a very high budget for comedy writers. We take the money that many shows give to dancers and put it in comedy writing.

I get together with Herbie on discussing the guest of that week and he and the writers come up with notions of what kind of sketch could be done with, say, Tim Conway or Lily Tomlin or Bill Cosby. Like: Lily Tomlin signs up with computer-dating. Flip wants a date. They find they are right for each other but the computer says no . . . Many times Herbie and the writers all work on the phone at night, when they will cook up an idea between them, a great idea. They'll work out the outline, Herbie will call me, and I'll okay the idea or not.

He and I work together a lot, though he's a great writer by himself. We spark each other an awful lot. I'm a great collaborator. It amazes me to find what I can get from other people. Not just Herbie, but Herbie is a particularly gifted writer. He is also a great procrastinator, which he knows. But we worked that out soon after he joined the show simply by my letting him know my expectations were high, and there was no time for procrastination. He didn't want to leave the show. He had a lot of special pride in it. He felt me and I felt him; I turned him on and he inspired me. So I really lean on him, give him a sense of responsibility, let him know every day is a deadline and check with him constantly, and he loves this kind of sense of responsibility. He works seven days a week. That's the great thing about what we have going here now. We draw on one of the most creative forces I've ever known, but it's a mutual process. I've gotten the best out of him. I know him; I just know him that well.

A: We've noticed that the team thing is very common among comedy writers. And you're talking about a sort of team-thing with Herbie.

H: Absolutely, and I reflect the dynamics of this team-approach myself. When you write a weekly television show, and you want to come up with great material every week, you don't have the luxury of waiting for an idea to work out by itself. Anything you get, you have to bounce off someone right away. You need another guy to take your notions. Some guys may have great ideas but they don't have the confidence. It takes the other guy to see if it's good. This guy—the second guy—can sometimes lead the first one astray, so that they both end up out on a limb. But you need that other person.

F: What about when you were producing your own stuff back at the Knickerbocker?

H: I used my audiences. I tried it out in front of their eyes. I also tried things out on my wife and family. Not unusual. "Honey, what do you think of this?" Also my wife happens to be a writer, basically focusing on special material.

F: Was she a writer before you first met?

H: Well, I told you I am good at bringing people out and I have a great record for encouraging women to work. I started Women's Lib years before that expression was coined. I encourage women to write, mostly because it's a great way for them to make points without having to go through the assembly-line deal.

About teams again. Many times one guy is the idea man; the other is the dialogue man. One comes up with great notions and the other knows how to put them into jokes. I can do both; I'm a little stronger on ideas. I can't compete with an ardent, sardonic comedy writer. I'm more the humanist, biting wit. They do jokes about this team thing at the writer's shows—we used to have them for kicks, kidding our own business. Sometime, the collaboration is good for just making sure you get started by ten in the morning. If a guy's on his own, it's easy to say, "First I'll go and talk to the gardener." Then talk to the unemployment agency, then remember he needs a haircut. The day flies by and he hasn't written a thing. But when he knows he has to meet John Doe at ten o'clock he shows up and starts writing. There are many teams where one guy makes money for just being a body. Sometimes the guy who is strong doesn't want another strong guy to compete with and he doesn't mind if he gives the other guy half the income just for being there—because otherwise he might get nothing.

There are so many excuses. It's so easy to go to the refrigerator. "I've got to check my competitors—watch the television." I have to go shopping or have a good dinner. "Time to take a nap." I've done it all. I'm speaking from real life.

A: I've always been interested in the team situation. When I wrote film, I wrote alone, and called people up on the phone to get their reactions. It must be important to have the response of a person right there in the room with you. It may even be a silent thing. You don't really have to *say*, "It's great." You could *feel* the feedback.

H: Yes. I am especially responsive to other people's reactions. So is Herbie. He may say to me, "I mentioned an idea to Hal (Goldman)." I can tell just by Herbie's face if Hal bought the idea. Let me level with you, and tell you something I couldn't have said about myself five years ago. On a previous show I worked on, I was having trouble working with my writers. I was writing, producing and directing the whole show. I did everything. Well, my analyst said, "The minute you stop trying to prove that you're a writer, then you really have to *be* a writer." It seems I had to *prove* to these guys that I was creative. Once

I stopped trying to prove it, the ideas got flowing. It was another great therapy session, that morning.

I stopped trying to prove how smart I was, how clever a writer I was. I listened more and could play a more subordinate role for them, even though I was the producer. I gave the writer a feeling he was taking over. Saying, "Why don't we do this?" would turn them off because they were the writers. Letting them go and reflecting off their stuff by "getting my edge in" would work much better. Like saying: "I like it a lot, it's a great idea, do you think maybe you'd do it in a trolley car instead of a train?" Let the writers feel they got the idea first. That helps, it's helped me to spark a lot of guys.

And working with a performer like Flip is fantastic, because like Shakespeare, taking old, old jokes and writing them in new ways, Flip will take all the creativity of a Herbie Baker and rework it to make it fit for him.

The two of us have a team-thing, too. I have to be able to tell him if his "way" is not quite right; to be diplomatic with the guy who is, after all, a great talent and the star of the show. He knows me by now to be a man of compassion; knows I don't want to hurt his feelings, and out of that kind of trust, he'll take another look at what he's doing.

Like me Flip is compelled to do a lot of rewriting. I'd rather have him over-write than under-write. We have a good thing. We work a whole day on turning down things to get one good idea.

We've been seen as twin brothers, by TV Guide. They said I am his white twin brother because we're the same size, we bounce instead of walk and our behinds stick out. It's incredible how we got thrown together, out of completely different backgrounds. I used to feel weird because I'm a shell-collector. He digs the ocean, too, goes to the beach and watches the sun go down, may sleep in the car. His idea of a good time is to meditate and so is mine. When he works Las Vegas, he'll finish the show at one and instead of hitting the booze or broads, he'll drive

out to the desert and see the sun rise. I love the desert,
too, the quiet moments . . . And, Flip has the same kind of
feeling for people as I do. He's a good analyst and a lover
of human nature. Neither of us do things the Hollywood
way.

I've never invited the stars over to socialize. I'm
never seen at Chasen's. I don't own a pair of suede shoes.
My hair is short. I have a real good time going to the
beach, wading in tide pools, and picking up my shells.

A girl I know, an associate producer, was listening
to me once telling someone I felt self-conscious about
these things. "How many guys with a national television
comedy show subscribe to *National Geographic* and
American Heritage?" I was saying. She overhead and said,
"That's what makes you so good. You open your mind to
everything, and somehow it works its way into your
show." Naturally, I liked to hear that; it was flattering. But
she's right, that's what I want to be, open to stimuli. Open
to people. She said: "You don't just see things as a show
biz guy; you open way up and comedy is life in the
mirror." I hope that's the way it is, because that's the way
I want it to be.

Summary

Throughout the interview with Bob Henry, he gives indication of his awareness of and deep concern about the
potentiality of hostility in humor. Two specific quotations
illustrate this attention: "We were all blessed with humor,
but I seemed to have come out 'way ahead of the others.
And it's continued to save my act in real life. Humor has
been a great cushion . . . "And, (Flip Wilson) knows me
by now to be a man of compassion, knows I don't want to
hurt his feelings . . . (he) has the same feeling for people
that I do. He's a good analyst and a lover of human
nature."

We could speculate at great length about where Bob derived his compassionate concern for others. His family apparently gave testimony to that quality when he was very young. His mother, who is characterized as a keen judge of people, listened to the young boy, "I seemed to have a kind of sageness or wisdom." He remembers admonishing his mother for "putting down" his brother.

We recognize that Bob had that quality already as a boy. Those childhood words evidence the same empathetic wisdom that later made him intuitively aware that he was more acceptable to Japanese audiences than were many other Americans. "I'm not a big guy, so I was no threat to them." Consistency is there, and gives strong evidence for the early development of this humanitarian quality.

Perhaps the quality derives from agony, and an attempt to minimize that agony. One could speculate that, since he hated for his family to be in a state of distress and unhappiness because of bitterness, nagging, dissatisfaction, and other forms of hostility, he honed his orientation toward compassion to a fine edge and became an advocate for humanitarian attitudes and behavior. This view would suggest that this quality in Bob's personality is something of an overcompensation or counter-reaction from the early environment.

But, if it is as simple as that: (my mother) "was ambitious and driving . . . She pushed everyone . . . My mother was the problem child in my life," then why didn't Bob Henry grow up to become a pushing nag, along the lines suggested by Leon Paul? "Those reared in such a way that they hate their parents will also hate other persons for life." Well, perhaps Bob was more strongly influenced by his father and modeled himself after that patient man. But the father was "fairly easy-going," "was content to be a barber," and was willing to think of going onto welfare. Bob doesn't evidence that more passive orientation to life.

With these considerations in mind, it becomes quite clear that no one-to-one explanation of Bob's humanitarian traits will be satisfactory, and will integrate all the information Bob has given us about his early life, his parents, and their behavior. Again, an attempt to find an easy answer to questions is thwarted.

Several years ago, scientists at the Menninger Clinic in Kansas carried out an experiment designed to explore the question of why medical doctors choose various medical specialties. The Menninger experimentation revealed that specialty choice is dictated, not by the pathologies of inner conflict, but by a doctor gravitating to a field where the required activities were most comfortable for him, and the least conflict-arousing.

There is a relevance of the Menninger study to Bob Henry's personality trait of compassionate concern about the hostile elements in life. Obviously, even from the years of his youth, Bob was comfortable about protesting man's inhumanity to man—he told his mother to get off his brother's back. At the beginning of his career he was already avoiding the sex-exploitation in his comedy material that constitutes most popular sexual humor. Only a few commonly distributed sexual jokes do not attack one or the other sex.

We are drawn to the conclusion that, probably for a number of complicated reasons, Bob was not oppressed by the same machismo orientation that forces so many other men into an antagonistic stance and inhibits their expressions of warmth and concern for the welfare of their fellow humans. Bob apparently experiences no hang-ups about being against hostility and violence; these positions create no demonstrable traumatic conflict for him.

Another factor to consider is the subject that links all of these professional writers with one another, and with all of us—authors and readers: humor. "Living through all this (family distress), there was a personal strain for me, for all of us. But through it all, through my mother's driving, on the back of my fairly easy-going father, there was always laughing."

Similarly, our other writers have mentioned this blessed boon of humor's coping effectiveness. The tension and irritability around Bob Henry's family dinner table was relieved by laughter. Humor provided a happy alternative to strain-producing behavior.

Bob's career demonstrates that, offered two alternatives—hostility and strain, or laughter and relief of tension—he has definitely opted for humor. That choice was already dormant in him that hot night in Boston when he told some jokes to entertain the night club patrons. The decision to prefer laughter carries with it the corollary of rejection of violence.

Another factor is quite evident in Bob's life which contributes to a rejection of violence. He was his family's wise man; he dispensed sage advice, even as a child. His mother asked his advice about a home heating unit. We don't know why he recommended coal, but presumably it was good advice. No doubt that by the time he started to log in his 1200 hours of psychotherapy, his orientation toward thinking things out was very strongly entrenched.

What is being considered here is the thinking, intellectual approach to dealing with life's problems and issues, rather than the simplistic, knee-jerk, bestial, violent approach—thinking things out rather than fighting them out—diplomacy and discussion rather than antagonism and attack. Granted; thinking things out can be infinitely more difficult than punching someone or shooting someone. But violence ultimately defeats our efforts, frustrates our hopes, and destroys those degrees of refinement which we have so laboriously, over so many centuries, built upon the foundation of our primitive heritage.

Humor—as created by Bob Henry and by all the other writers studied here, as well as by all other writers and comedians and clowns and jesters and performers and entertainers, and by all the rest of us—is not the only agent whereby intelligence and good will and love work to offset the elements of violence in the world—but it is one of the most common and it is one of the most effective.

Billy Barnes

Comedy and Cadence—
Rhythm is the
Score of Humor

BILLY BARNES was born in Los Angeles in 1934. He
went to U.C.L.A. and has been writing professionally
since 1957. His hobbies are painting, travel, and dance.

His background includes his own enormously suc-
cessful stage revues in Los Angeles, as well as having
written special material for the Danny Kaye Show, Laugh-
In, Dean Martin's Summer Show, and specials for Dinah
Shore, Diana Ross, Bing Crosby, Alan King, Goldie Hawn,
to name a few. He is the composer of "Too Long at the
Fair," "Something Cool" and "Does Anybody Here Love
Me?" popularized by Barbra Streisand, June Christy and
Ann Margret, respectively. He is proud possessor of six
Emmy nominations and vows, "I'm going to keep doing it
until I get it right."

One of the unexpected thrills in this study was the discovery of the importance of music in a comedy writer's life. Nearly all the writers interviewed reported fairly extensive contact with music, at least during childhood. Several writers have produced professional musicians in the younger generation of their families. Herbie Baker was practically born to the onstage singing of his show business mother. Ruth Flippen sang and danced professionally as a tiny "Baby Ruth" at the age of three years.

The subject of the following interview manifests the heaviest investment in music among our writers. Billy Barnes was put to the piano at a tender age, became a family entertainment institution as a juvenile, and started writing musical comedy in high school. The major part of his career consists of a combination of music and humor—as Billy puts it: his "shows," his "ditties," his "revues," his "little things," his "musicals." In this interview he vividly describes the intense interaction between humor and music during his creative activity.

Several years ago, one of us (Fry) began a collection of material relating to a hypothetical association of comedy and music. The hunch that prompted this data pack-ratting was sparked by a comment attributed to musician Bill Haley, leader of the rock music group The Comets, "Music is supposed to be for happiness, to make people *laugh*, to make them dance." Later, dancer Martha Graham added further stimulus in her remark, "I like to do comedy (in dance) . . . You have to have something that makes you treasure joy to do comedy."

Joy may be one feature shared by both humor and music, but it emerges from numerous diverse sources that there are many other factors indicating an uncommon degree of association between them. Among these, certainly rhythm must be most prominent. In his classic book *Soundmaking*, psychiatrist Peter Ostwald describes rhythm as one of the basic biological attributes.

It is more cliché than profundity to express that rhythm has vital importance to music. Less recognized but not completely news is the fact that rhythm has vital importance in humor. Considerations of rhythm in humor are generally collected under the rubric of *timing*. Most of us are aware of the great importance of timing in joke-telling, of the timing that may be essential for the precipitation of mirth during some event of real life, and of the special art in timing cultivated by talented professional comedians. Sociologist Arthur Asa Berger reminds us of that highlight in radio entertainment during a Jack Benny program. A robber accosts Benny with "your money or your life." Paaauuuusssseeeeee. Finally the robber demands, "Well?!" To which Benny replies, "I'm thinking! I'm thinking!"

The timing, or rhythm in that exchange is especially crucial. Even before the spoken punchline, "I'm thinking! I'm thinking!" is delivered, an initial punchline is presented in the lengthening pause. As the pause extends longer and longer, underlining the miser's conflict of priorities, more and more people begin laughing. Timing, itself, becomes the joke. The statement about "I'm thinking"—a good enough punchline on its own merits—becomes part of a tandem punchline, with the preceding pause. This joke is an outstanding example of the significance of timing to humor, in that tandem-punchline jokes, as a group, are particularly sensitive to the influence of timing, and this specific example utilizes timing as an explicit part of the punchline.

Several comedy writers in this group describe themselves as "born" humorists. It is reasonable to assume that these remarks are directed at a talent for being "ridiculous." This talent is itself not so ridiculous as it is creative. The writers are describing, in actuality, a heightened capacity for being able to bring forth from the implicit shadow-world of mental symbols and associations those concepts which are both appropriate and inappropriate to the preceding content of the joke or humorous life situation. They are thus revealed as being intelligent and sensitive and wise in their understanding of the issues of life. They evidence an innate grasp of human psychology. The "born" humorist must know intuitively what themes will take form in the minds of his audience in response to certain "story" content. One, or a combination of these themes will provide the content of the appropriate-inappropriate punchline—appropriate, in the sense that the audience will comprehend and feel the association; inappropriate, in the sense that the audience has not recognized the association in its collective minds until the punchline delivery, and thus learns something new about life and about themselves individually.

It is reasonable, also, to assume that describing oneself as a "born" humorist is a statement about a deep-seated sense of timing. These professional writers make quite clear, through one remark and another, that proper timing in humor is more than knowing the best length of a pause to stimulate the greatest mirth, or the most laughter-provoking rate for one joke to follow another. Rhythm is the underlying organization of the entire humorous item—be it of real life or a product of the entertainment world. The cadence is the skeleton of the body; it is the frame of the building. Upon this internal structure is developed the individuality of each humorous episode, through its words and actions. Beneath the conceptual content is a rhythm, or timing, that is necessary —as in music—for the episode to "come off," to evoke the quintessence of mirth.

In discussing this innate talent for timing, we run into the boringly recurrent question of heredity vs. environment, nature vs. nurture. Is this talent a genetic gift? Are these professionals endowed by a generous Mother Nature with a gift for especially attentive communion with a universal cadence found in less developed degree in other humans? Or, is the humorist with superb timing a beneficiary of strong childhood exposure to some source of rhythmic beat which impresses its throbbing pattern into his habits of cognition and feeling? Does his proclivity for music and his proficiency in creating humor indicate a heightened household sensitivity to the various cadences of life?

We would like to think that it is not so simple that the cause can be traced to one or to the other. At least five million years of direct evolutionary development have brought mankind to his contemporary state. One would hope that such an auspicious lineage grants better than an 'either/or' mechanism.

Rhythm in music lends character to the music, and is a significant determinant of its impact upon the listener. The timing of a procession of notes has a major influence on the mood and mental associations stimulated by the sounds. Joyful music has a lively cadence; dirges are slow. Passion, anger, tenderness, and many other emotions are stimulated, and conveyed, by rhythm. With speech, a similar finding is made. The rhythm of speech is an important component of the communication process. Actors and public figures deliberately train in these matters.

Abstractly, musical rhythm can be analyzed as two separate phenomena interacting together. Rhythm is established by a sequence of sounds separated by silent intervals of varying lengths. The sounds are components of a discontinuous phenomenon, and are imposed onto a continuous phenomenon—which is time. This analysis may be restated to define music as a digital phenomenon—sound—imposed upon the temporal continuity. It is the relationship between these two which establishes the rhythm. This same elementary description can be applied to speech and to laughter. Human humor, through operation of its punchline paradox, transcends this basic relationship, in that human perception of the continuity of time is exploded by this paradox. However, until the punchline delivery, and the precipitation of its, "This is unreal" paradox, the timing—or rhythm—is crucial.

Studies by Neurophysiologist Manfred Clynes purport to add rigor to descriptions of the relationship between musical rhythm and emotions. Dr. Clynes has presented evidence for existence in humans of a cross-cultural system (Sentics) of action-forms (actons) and concepts (idiologs). The two are related according to a pattern that indicates a distinct acton uniquely associated with each distinct idiolog. For example, the emotion of joy will be universally and consistently experienced in association with a characteristic movement impulse (esentic form). Dr. Clynes has recorded these movement impulses by measuring the rhythm of muscular pressure of a single finger, while the subject concentrates on a specific idiolog.

Various other experimental findings imply both innate, genetic rhythmic phenomena built into the human organism, and innate sensitivities to influences by external rhythm.

Manifested by these findings, and others, is both a "music of the spheres" and a music from within. We emanate our rhythms out to the universe, as its rhythms are randomly reflected onto us. This profound impact of rhythm in human life could be taken, with flight of fancy, as lending verisimilitude to the Hindu religious tradition that the god Siva creates the rhythms of the Universe by the intensity of his dancing. Siva dances the cosmic dance, and darkness is illuminated. Life is created, order is made of chaos by the pulsing energy of his cadence radiated into eternity. Rebirth and annihilation of all things are controlled by the radiations of this rhythm.

More concrete is the knowledge recently established by brain studies that, for a right-handed person, activity of the right cerebral hemisphere of the brain is more intense when listening to music, than is activity of the left hemisphere. (The picture is rather more complicated for left-handed people.) The two hemispheres are described as having two different cognitive 'styles.' The style of the right hemisphere is characterized as holistic, nonlinear, associative, based on the propensity for developing concepts from multiple converging determinants, rather than linear and logical analysis as is the case for the left hemisphere. (A review of these studies is found in neuropsychiatrist David Galin's article, *Implications for Psychiatry of Left and Right Cerebral Specialization,* Archives of General Psychiatry, Volume 31, 1974.) It is apparent that this holistic style is necessary for comprehension of rhythm. What would holistically be recognized as rhythm, would to a linear brain be apparent simply as a sequence of stimuli, without pattern. The left brain hears the notes; the right brain hears the music.

This sidedness applies also to the experience of humor, and that fact may say something about the common importance of rhythm to both humor and music. The left hemisphere perceives and comprehends the words and other symbols of humor, but the right hemisphere is the side that puts together the concepts and the association of ideas brought about by the humor content. David Galin described right hemisphere function, "It is much superior to the left in part-whole relations, grasping the concept of the whole from just a part . . . it deals more effectively with complex patterns taken as a whole than with the individual parts taken serially . . . The elements in these verbal constructions do not have fixed single definitions, but depend on context, and can shift in meaning when seen as parts of a new pattern." Essential characteristics of the 'language' of humor are easily recognized in Dr. Galin's description.

This function of the right hemisphere seems pertinent to comments by Billy Barnes during the following interview, "When I start to create . . . It opens something and it comes. If I ponder it, it's never any good; because then I get too involved and too clever . . . It's like in paradise and the mind starts working, which is most exciting." We know that the two hemispheres of the brain do not operate independently of one another, unless serious pathology has occurred. A division of labor exists between the hemispheres. At any particular time, during any particular function, one hemisphere is dominant over the other. As he creates, Billy certainly doesn't turn *off* his left hemisphere, but perhaps that "opening" is a switching *into* right hemisphere dominance. To be sure, a style of mental functioning in which rhythm perception is significant must dominate when both music and humor are experienced.

We stated earlier that musical rhythm is established by the relationship between a digital stimulus—sound —and temporal continuity. We added that the same observation could be applied to laughter. There are some interesting considerations about laughter that have to do with this business of comedy and cadence.

Laughter is one of the few remaining nonverbal tribal vocalizations. It shares this distinction with crying, humming, roaring (such as a crowd at a sports event), keening, screaming, moaning, and sounds of sexual passion. At least three of the higher primates—man, chimpanzees, and gorillas—exhibit laughter. And, in the case of man, this nonverbal, rhythmic vocalization exists as a major behavior despite the dominence of verbal behavior.

Laughter can be thought of as akin to choral music, a tribal song without words. But, laughter in chorus is a *shared* song—a blend of many individual parts, rather than a song in unison. Each person has his or her own individual style of laughter. Unseen, a person can be recognized as much from the sound of his laughter as from other vocalizations. A large number of variable qualities enter into this capacity of humans to produce characteristically individual laughter, one quality being that of rhythmicity. There are, in laughter, many rhythms. There are the rhythms of the component parts of laughter (expiration, inspiration, pause), the rhythms of magnitudes of sound and air passage, the rhythms of various subpatterns within the broader laughter episode. Individual variation of laughter creates the resultant situation that each person's laughter is a personal monogram, affirming that person's unique selfness.

Billy Barnes, and all his comedy-writing colleagues, are creating opportunities for mirth—but they are also contributing far more. They are writing scores for a sort of universal music, a tribal cadence that resounds deep within the human mind. They are also preparing librettos for each individual who is audience to their humor, that those individuals may sing, in their laughter, their personal aria of unique identity. Small wonder their talent is cherished.

Interview

Fry: Can you tell us something about how you got into the entertainment world? Where were your first jobs, how did you find them? How did you break into the field?

Barnes: Actually it started in college. I had always played the piano. I could never sing very well, but I used to love to write songs to sort of get at it. I wrote some shows in junior high school. When I went to college, UCLA, I started doing shows, and that led rather logically into working with the same group I had worked with in college into little theaters in L.A.

F: What shows were you doing in college?

B: I was studying Theater Arts at UCLA at the time, and for Creative Workshop No. 55, a friend of mine had found a book he wanted to make into a musical comedy. It was a very funny little revue. I didn't know what a revue was, but he asked, would I write the music for it? He had heard me at parties doing my little ditties, Noel Coward and other goodies. And so I said, fine. We put the thing on, and it was quite a success. It was done in the theater in the round, and the department saw it and liked it. Ralph Freud liked it and wanted to be starred in it, which I loved. They then put it on as the main stage production that term—and so that was my first musical. Then I wrote another show which we never put on, and a third one, which was put on at Stanford University, with a huge production. It was marvelous, and I went to see it, but I had nothing to do with the production.

Allen: How old were you then, Bill? About when was this?

B: I think "Footprints"—which was the college show—was 1948.

A: You said you did things earlier, in junior high also?

B: Yeah, considerably earlier than that, about 1943. This is interesting that you should bring this up. I recently saw Frank Sinatra at a benefit for Dinah Shore. He was marvelous, and I remembered the first real comedy song I ever wrote in high school was called "Just Call Me Frankie" about Frank Sinatra. Then I began to remember school assemblies and the like, when everyone got loud and funny, and the kind of material I used to write.

B: The show I wrote for the Stanford production was a book show, a story—a comedy. I wrote the book, then a fellow picked the book up and I wrote the songs. After I got out of college I did piano playing in bars and had an act, and used to write comedy material for the act. I had worked in college with a divine guy named Bob Rogers. He appeared in two of the shows I wrote in college, and we were very good friends. We all got together with this friend I'd heard was opening a night club in Palm Springs. I gathered together this nucleus of kids and we decided we were going to do a night club act with Kay Thompson, who discovered the Williams Brothers. In night clubs, at the time, they were customarily doing sophisticated lyrics. But I started writing material and went on and on, like young people do, never editing. It just went on until we had this little capsule revue for about thirty-five minutes. There were five of us. We auditioned at several clubs in Palm Springs with our little act, and Sammy Davis, Jr., who was completely unknown then, was appearing with his family at the Chi Chi. He saw our audition and flipped and told us, "You guys must be hired," like he still is today, the most dynamic guy in the world. And we got hired, these dumb kids from college, and we were doing all this chic British stuff. It was awful, we lasted one show. It was a supper show, people were eating and we felt we were charming; a smash, you know. The people were talking and by the end of that show the owner said you're too sophisticated for our crowd, and that ended it.

Afterward, Bob and I started to write sketches. He'd write the talk and I'd write the music. Then we went to New York, I got married, and came back here, and he stayed on. When my wife and I separated, he came back to L.A. and that is when he said "put all of your stuff together and call it a revue." So we put it all together in 1956 and had a concert in Los Angeles. We made $10 a week, but it was our first professional theater experience.

That was the first Cabaret concert show. I rehearsed it, but I was regularly working the piano bar. I had to make money. Bob edited and directed it, and made all the contacts. One of his contacts knew everybody in the world, so we got all the Industry down there. It was amazing, the very first thing we ever did. It was a good show, we rehearsed and rehearsed until we really knew what we were doing. That was a half hour show. We used to do it in three sections in this particular club. They started us on as a curtain opener, and we were a sensation. So they got rid of the other act and we did the whole evening. That's when I thought, "gee"—so I started writing more and filling in the sections until it was an hour and a half show each evening—then two hours. We got that on and more people kept coming back. In '58 Jack Benny came down to see the show and hired us for Gisele McKenzie, the ill-fated television half hour. So we wrote on that, and that was our first professional television writing job. We were working the next Monday. We did that whole television season.

Also, the revue had moved many places. We went to Ciro's, the Interlude, we did tab versions of it. We went to the Hungry I, which was very exciting. But we couldn't go with it any more, Bob and I. After the television job folded, we went back to the revue whole-heartedly, went to the Las Palmas, and then New York and London and Florida. We kept doing the revues. We were endlessly funny and getting poorer and poorer. And finally we just weren't making enough money, and I owed back income taxes. All of a sudden a man by the name of Nick Vanoff came walking in when we were doing the Billy Barnes L.A.—I think in '64—and the next day we were doing a special Bing Crosby, Frank Sinatra—huge special, gorgeous, an hour and a half, and we were treated like the two best writers in the world. And that led to Danny Kaye. One of the guys who worked with me on the Bing Crosby show was looking for a writer replacement, blah, blah. I got the show—for the next 3½ years. That was the really solid start.

F: We are getting into a different area here. Actually, I want to ask you what sort of relationship you ordinarily have with the comedian you are working for.

B: When I worked for Danny Kaye, whom I really respected, and he was going through, "I want to do my funny period. I don't want any fast numbers or double-talk." And I thought, Oh, my God, what are we going to write for him? So I had to get to know him, because the first three numbers I wrote, I heard, "I don't do that any more." I wrote two numbers, one was a monstrous thing which I lived to see Danny finally do. I had to do both numbers, and they were really kind of good.

But really, in order to write a comedy song—the hardest thing in the world to write, as far as I'm concerned, in my field, is a stand-up solo performer comedy number. Group numbers are the easiest to write. With a great scene—I can take pollution—I know I could sit down and write ten numbers on that right now. Or campus unrest—those kinds of things—women's fashions. Those are easy, all for a group of people, because it's sort of a production number. But solo! They first have to have an attitude, and you have to know pretty well what they're selling. Women always seem to be the same. They have what people want to be funny. I don't know why. Men always have their bag of tricks.

It's easy when you know the guy. Danny Kaye has an overload of talent. And a Carol Channing, you know damned well she is going to bring so much more than you ever thought about, with her eyes rolling. That's heaven for a comedy writer; for me, anyway. Music has a way of lulling the mind a bit, you know. I always used to get mad when we'd write a revue. I'd write these funny songs, I'd think, and then we'd put a little section in the middle where they'd talk. It would become a musical scene. The talk got all the laughs. But when you get a tempo going, and a rhythm, they only laugh at the rhymes and block out. I always think they can hear everything.

And also, when you write lyrics, I find, you are trying to be clever sometimes instead of funny, because I'm working for a rhyme. You wait for the rhyme in the comedy number when you wouldn't in a folk song.

F: Like Gilbert and Sullivan.

B: I still think it's where it is laughwise.

A: What about yourself as a younger person, did you dig funny things then?

B: Yes, it's funny how it all started—it seems now like it has been forever, when I think back. I just recently bought some Judy Garland posters, and I thought, my gosh, that's how it all started, in a way, because I still love those old movies. I still identify with Mickey Rooney. When the kids I played with as a boy got together, we would come out and sing those great big silly songs, do impressions and things. We loved that.

But even before then, I played piano. My mother taught me when I was six. I took lessons formally at seven. And it seemed that I was always making up little things for the piano. I remember vividly when I started being very serious. We were doing a show in junior high school. I had seen Tin Pan Alley—I loved Betty Grable. I practically paraphrased that number, and thought "We'll do it in the revue at school." I don't know what we called it—"All You Singers" or something. I did this huge number and everybody was so surprised that I could do this. That's how my particular thing started. We started doing shows in school and we'd do (this was during the war) things about food stamps, gasoline stamps, about all those fantastic sexy ladies, Rita Hayworth, etc. And everything was all fun, a sort of take-off.

I really always wanted to be an actor and performer. But at the time everyone wanted to be in the limelight, and it was easier to go to the piano and start writing these little things and then give them to someone else to perform and play the piano for them.

F: As you started out you had both humor and music.

B: I remember when I got to college, the first day, in acting class, I had to stand up in Acting I, or whatever it was called, and say what I really wanted to do. I guess you were supposed to say "acting." I said, "I'm going to write Broadway musicals like Cole Porter." It just kind of came out. Immediately, I thought I had better sit down and shut up. But it was the first time I admitted to myself that this was the kind of thing I wanted to do. Later, in the service—I was in for a short time, in the Navy—I was writing shows all the time, but always these unrelated hunks.

A: Maybe we could go back. What was the structure of your family when you were a kid?

B: My father was a mechanic, but he had always wanted to sing. He was very uneducated, must have gone to about the sixth grade. But he always had a rather fine side to him. He always loved the theater, although he couldn't participate. He took singing lessons when he was very young, when he married my mother, and he really sang a lot. Never sang professionally, but sang around at weddings and things, and mother played the piano. She had such a love for the piano. She was self-taught. She played for him to sing. They would sing at parties. When I was three, I was so terribly shy—Mother was telling us the other day, and I felt like hitting her. I was introverted to the point I was never going to do anything, so they decided dancing lessons were the answer. Why, I'll never know, and—the Meglin kiddies—I mentioned Meglin in an interview, and Mrs. Meglin wrote me a letter. She couldn't remember me—she had thirty schools. But I was happy there, I went four sessions and I wouldn't leave her side. Finally my grandmother, who was a swinger, said "Get out there and dance, honey." She threw me out there. I did my Indian thing. Mother said recently, "He was performing when he was three years old, but then he got measles and we never could get him on stage again."

But anyway, my father's dream—my mother was the practical one—my father had these dreams that I shouldn't dirty my hands. He was always working with his hands on cars. He insisted on these lessons, so I took singing lessons and piano lessons. My teacher was very nice because she never demanded that I do things, she always let me express whatever I wanted to do, although the lessons were all classical. It was a classical training. I could come in and say, "Gosh, I wrote this thing," and she'd say, "Fine—now we must go back to Bach," or something. I knew right away I was never going to be a classical pianist. I would play pop music. My friends—we used to act in the backyard. My family loved theater and all that, but they weren't theatrical, we weren't a show biz family or anything.

A: Was your family funny?

B: Not particularly. My father was Irish. I've always thought he had a great gift for lyrics. He could make up poems right out of his head, and he could go on forever. I loved words from him, I loved music from Mother. She was a forceful influence. She said she sat next to me at the piano for three solid years and never let me up. My grandmother was really funny. My mother's mother. I really admired her. She was the life of the party type. As soon as I got the piano down pretty good, when I was about eight and a half, all these parties that were so popular in the 30s, before I went to bed, I'd have to play. Pretty soon I could play for people to sing at the parties. The minute I got behind the piano, I was funny. I was always looking to entertain. My mother would take over at my bedtime. Soon I aced her out, she said. Finally, I played all night. I remember one time I didn't want to play and my father said he was going to beat me up if I didn't. They were a bit much in that area. I remember I was crying, or something, saying that he was taking the joy out of my playing. Then I got morbid—a wall was built around me, but I was already becoming the thing behind the piano. And I loved—I didn't really, but I thought I did—to get attention.

F: We would be interested in your customary pattern of creation. For example, do you start writing at night time or do you start in the morning? Where do you do your writing?

B: I do it usually, my best work, when I'm terribly pressured. If I have a week—I'll go to the beach for six days and on the seventh I'll get panicked. But I've been thinking, I've been talking to friends of mine. People don't understand—that funk you go into when you're really thinking. So on the seventh day I start thinking more and more. It's very difficult for me to concentrate, and I find things like phones and weather and people get in my way. I don't go to an office, I've made that clear, I have to say "No, I do it at home." I have to have that kind of fanatical thing. I don't answer phones, I won't talk, I won't get a drink. I'll just sit.

F: Where?

B: I sit in my den. It's weird, I have a piano that my mother had when she was young. I don't know how many years old it is, but I have always known this piano. I learned to play on it—it was the only piano we had. I have dragged around this old, ancient, and now I think it's beginning to be antique piano, that I love. But I can only write on it. I finally bought my first baby grand. I was so thrilled. And I have an electric piano, but I have never composed anything except on that old piano. I sit there and think "I could play something on this one." So I usually write it and then come in and play it for myself, record it on my tape recorder, also. I've always played on that piano. I feel it's lucky and I feel at home with it. I have it tuned, and it still plays great.

When I start to create, the tune is the easiest part of it. It almost just comes. It's weird, but it is almost God-given, it just comes. It opens something and it comes. If I ponder it, it's never any good; because then I get too involved and too clever. I may think that I want it to be involved, to take time. But I will worry it too much, and get it too complicated and they can't sing it well. So I now use a little cassette tape recorder for my very first run—like I don't know what this will be, but it'll come to me. And

I'll turn on the tape recorder and sit at the piano, and I never play it back because once I know, it's there. At times, I've written so many so fast—it sounds like salami. I sometimes laugh, but it'll be there. I've never not had it on that deadline night, I can stay up all night.

A: How many songs on an average a week are you writing now?

B: Well, let's say three. Sometimes I'll do a whole lot. I can't do more than five, and that's working all the time. This deadline thing is sometimes so extreme that I've written on the way to the studio, which is closer to the line than I like to be.

A: Just before you start writing the lyrics, when you're sitting down at your old piano, what goes on inside of you?

B: I like to write. I don't know why it is, but it seems like five a.m. is when I turn on. I usually get feverish. I get feeling very good. I get glassy-eyed, and I sit in this leather chair by the piano with my spiral notebook. I have to write the words on a certain spiral notebook. Oh, God, I don't know if I *have* to, but I do. I sit there and I don't move. It's like in paradise and the mind starts going, which is most exciting. I suppose I could do it every day if I were panicked or pressured. I'm constantly running back and forth to the piano; I can't sit at the piano, and I don't write out the notes until later. I do that in my head. I'm working on the lyrics all the time. Then I run to the piano, and it's so funny because I have to sing and talk—I have to perform it, because I know it doesn't work unless I do. Sometimes I may think what I've written is so funny on paper and then I get up and it isn't funny at all in performance because the words aren't coming in the right place. I have to really sing it. I remember I once had a house guest and I couldn't work at all because I was embarrassed—especially because I try to sound like the person I'm writing for—like Mae West or Danny Kaye, or whoever. I can get really tickled by what I'm writing, and I laugh, I get—oh, God, that's so good, I can't stand it. If I think it's funny, I like it. I approve many times of what I do.

F:　Do you remember any particular occasion when you really got carried away?

B:　Oh, yes. I wrote a number for a show a long time ago, but I remember I was screaming and laughing. It's still a show-stopper. It's called—you may have heard it—about a woman who sold popcorn, and the guy's line was "her popcorn's fairly fresh," which I really didn't think anything about. I thought it was a funny title, I guess. But I started to write it and it became almost obscene. I don't know why, but I got on that kick, and you take a simple thing like popcorn and it turns into standing for her charms, and everything gets a little naughty —everything having to do with popcorn. Like, "Maybe a little old, well, but with melted butter, who can tell?" It just got very *double entendre*, and it had a lot of funny sounds in it. I think it is the wonder of lyrics. In our language—it works. You want it so say something, and these two words rhyme and of all the words in the whole world, why did those two fall into place right then? It's marvelous. It's like a puzzle, and you finally have some answers.

F:　You were talking about the piano and the notebook and leather chair. Do you have any other special aids in accentuating this burst of creativity, like religion or any particular recreation that you'll engage in for the day or two days beforehand, or any ritual?

B:　There isn't any particular ritual. A typical pattern for me is to wake up in the morning and put it off and put it off. I'll go to a movie, I'll do anything but sit down and do it. Finally at 5 a.m., when I sit down and do it, I don't know why I have ever done anything else. Say, I'll want to write a march and I can't even remember what a march is like, for God's sake. I'll go in and maybe put on a Robert Preston record from "Music Man." I start listening to that, and sort of get excited. The mood may change and I'll play all kinds of records during this time. I can't steal from them; but I just want to get that feeling. Sometimes I'll use just certain records that—like Barbra Streisand, it's not her voice I hear, but she has such excitement and theatricality that I can start feeling something and I'll run to the piano and start going. I do that a lot.

As far as preparing for writing—I'd never shave to write. At 5 a.m. I'm usually in nylon pajamas, and they have to be nylon, or I'd be happy if I didn't wear any clothes at all. I usually wear swimming trunks in summer and in winter I wear pajamas, and I'll wear them all day.

A: Are you up the night before or are you getting up at 5 a.m.?

B: I get up. That night, I go to bed and I can't sleep because I know I'm going to get up. That feverish thing of mine keeps going 'round and 'round and I'll stay awake and go mad and then sit down and it starts. Oh, it's like an IBM machine, brrr, and such a fitful night. Usually, then I run in to work and I'll have to play it, do it, whatever, writing the words. It's a wonder I don't kill people, as I drive to the studio, I'm so nervous. Every week I can't imagine what I put myself through, this sweating. I get so nervous for fear they're going to be rejected.

A: You still do?

B: Oh, yes, always. And if it is rejected, I'm up all night again, because it has to be done. They give you 24 hours, and that's it, and then you have to go into rehearsal. And that's an awful feeling. I've bombed about four times in three years, so that's not bad. But the thought of it scares me to death. And usually if I think, "Boy, they're going to love it," that's the one I'm nervous about. But if I go the other way, "I *think* it's good, I hope they like it," then it's usually—*whee!* I usually feel kind of groovy, after I'm sweating. I get what I expect, I pretty well know if it's really good. If it's sort of good, I hope they'll like it a little better, and if it's kind of bad I get defensive.

F: Do you think you're funny, Billy?

B: No. Oh, sometimes I think I'm pretty funny, but I think I should be a lot funnier than I am. I get very moody

and depressed, recently—I don't know why. I was thinking that humor is pretty darned important. I've always felt
the most marvelous way to say things first is to music, and
second through comedy. I think you can say almost anything because music is universal and almost everyone digs
that, and I always thought cartoons and fairy tales were
marvelous because you could almost say anything. That's
why I think writing comedy is kind of fulfilling, because all
along I think I've been able to say little things I wanted to
get out of my system—hasty things. You can say things
and then put it to music and it makes the pill a little easier
to swallow. And the rhymes make it a little happy, and I
feel it's terribly important. I sometimes wish I could be a
more serious composer—more of a poet. And yet when
Laurence Olivier and Maggie Smith are at their best,
they've always got that humor coming through. And I
guess I'm just as happy that that's what I do.

A: What about in your social life? You said you don't
think you're funny all the time. Do you think of humor as
a form of environment you're in?

B: When I'm with funny people. I like comedy actors.
Some comediennes are not really funny at all—they're
tormented human beings socially. But nice comical actors
and writers—writers are the funniest, except they're
overwhelming to me. I just sit there and laugh at them.
They break me up. I like to laugh. I do find, and I've been
letting myself go more toward being what I think all the
time—kind of fun—just to kind of be myself and be silly if
I want to be.

F: Some of the longer things you've written suggest
that you've made observations about changing styles or
maybe raised some questions about regional humor
—comedy that will meet the tastes of people in one part of
the country as well as other parts of the country. Do you
have any thoughts about this?

B: The thing I like most about the regional thing is the
sound. It kills my ears. I get a kick out of that. The whole
thing is this new humor. I guess it's new humor. I just
loved Lennie Bruce. It's sick, and I don't write that way,

but thinking back, he just utterly floored me when I first saw him in person. I had to be carried out. Then Jonathan Winters still absolutely devastates me with the sounds again. He makes those wonderful characters.

But I'm appalled at my son and what he thinks is funny. Now, with me, of course, he goes my way. He says the funniest things. I was saying something to him the other day—he's seventeen, and not a child—and he's been around it forever. But he was saying something, and I said something scathing to him about his long hair or something, and he said, "God, with your mouth, you ought to make money saying those things." And I said, "Darling, I do." He came back with, "I keep forgetting that's what you do."

But he'll talk to me on a different level, and we'll get to laughing and making up silly things. He's got great ears for words and everything.

I guess when you come right down to it—simply enough—it helps to laugh a little.

Summary

Billy Barnes could be a perfect subject for another go-around on the old nature-nurture controversy. After reading his interview, you may feel as we do that it is a very complex picture of how Billy "got that way." He came into adulthood secure in the knowledge that being the party-entertainer pays off handsomely—both professionally and in terms of personal fulfillment.

Let us give you a picture of Billy. First of all, he bubbles constantly. He seems to live as he creates, with a kind of nonstop, catchy, dynamic meter. He is really with you when you are with him, and you are soon caught up in his intensity. Time flies along in this sustained peaking of experience. Billy, looking a bit like an eternal leprechaun—elfin and quick—is a giant among men in his charismatic impact. He is the wise little boy who has now become a youthful-looking wise man. One senses he holds the keys and he freely lets you use them. He is as interested in our field as we are in his. He is generous with his life, giving himself to us fully in the short amount of time we had with him.

As we have discussed, there are two types of humorists—performers and more subdued types. In making this delineation, however, we do not want to indicate that all writers who seem to be "on" in real life have similar basic personalities.

Billy would certainly fit into the performer category, but his "performance" is entirely without self-conciousness. You get the feeling that life is, in a sense, a series of funny sketches for Billy, and that he picks up on his environment constantly and totally without needing to think about it. Life as it is happening is material for the creative process, and this process, as it exists in Billy, is continuous and limitless. So one gets the feeling—not of the star—but of a person so turned-on to what is happening around him that he cannot help but elaborate on it, seizing it up and playing with it. There is nothing pretentious about him in the least. What he does comes off naturally and makes being with Billy simply a ball.

So we have the adult version of the little lad at the piano who gets enough positive external reinforcement so that he does not need to search for more. His conditioning seems to have led him to believe that life is as full as his participation in it.

Billy is a prime example for considerations of cadence and rhythm. He experienced from his early years the significance of music as a part of daily life, through his father, mother, grandmother, and the audiences of adults, and schoolmates. He, the boy-jester, incorporated the rhythm of all of this so that, as an adult, he moves cathodically, and speaks cathodically. He is a symbol, as he exists, of the dynamism of rhythm and pacing.

His sense of having always been in the business is one which Billy shares with some of our other writers —notably Ruth Flippen and Herbie Baker. There was no "breaking into the business"; it just seemed to follow in a natural flow.

Any failures he experienced early in his career seem to have been minor—learning experiences in that they led him to focus more precisely on doing what he was good at, so that when his first revue opened it was immediately recognized as a hit, and by some of the greats in show business. Billy speaks nostalgically about this instant success, and recaptured the sense of surprise he felt at that success occurring as it did when he was so young. He is able to say, not with bragadoccio, but with pride, "we were a sensation." Billy is a man who knows his talent, lays it out there, but just as a part of his patter.

Nothing about him suggests conceit; instead he has a kind of capricious whimsy, blended with his serious knowledge that he is good at what he does. It is very difficult to separate him—his being—from what he does. Billy has achieved what musician Bill Haley felt was essential in good music: the combination of music and humor. Billy has a quick wit and an intellect of high sophistication without thinking of himself as an intellectual. He has power, and he uses it positively—for himself—for others. In the verse and chorus of his dialogue there is a consistent theme: yes, he is a music-maker; yes, he is a humor-maker; but above all, he is a life-maker.

Recognizing his urge to be the center of things as an actor, he realistically coped with the fact that "at that time everyone wanted to be in the limelight," and stayed with the piano—a natural for him, and a site of special talent. The combination of humor and music is a synthesis for Billy that seems so integral as to be automatic.

It is interesting that, as a product of a father who was a "singing mechanic" and a mother who played for the father, Billy felt so shy at the age of three when his mother pushed him in the direction of show business with the well-known (in Los Angeles) Meglin Kiddies that he "felt like hitting her." His frustrated, naturally lyrical father wanted the "best" for his son. Billy spoke of his Dad hoping Billy would never have to "dirty his hands" the way he had had to. Words came from his father, and he learned to love music from his mother. The image of his mother sitting next to him at the piano ("she never let me up") is a powerful one.

As has been the case with several other writers in this book, Billy, too, had a grandmother "who was really funny." So, Billy had it all within his own household; he had all of the pieces and he put them together in his own inimitable way. The basic quality of the rhythmic component was already exhibited in the facility of young Billy, playing for adult parties at eight years of age, staying up at night to entertain, his mother being relegated to "second pianist." And, by this time, Billy was liking it. "The minute I got behind the piano, I was funny. I was always looking to entertain." The young son, originally pushed against his will into performing, subsequently replaced the "pusher"—his own mother.

The one sad note in this joyful spurt of autobiography was when he looked back and briefly viewed himself as "the thing behind the piano." He winced as he remembered that on one occasion when he hadn't wanted to play, his father had threatened to beat him. ("They were a bit much in that area.") Yet, as he fumbled with how he felt at that moment, verging on the morose, Billy suddenly shot up through it, trying to reconcile old ambivalences, saying, "I loved—I didn't really, but I thought I did—to get attention." One of us (Allen) wanted to take time out at that moment to do some soothing, to remind Billy that he could have felt both—the love of the attention and hate for the toll it cost him—and that the tremendous ambivalence young children feel in such situations is quite normal. But we were never "shrinks" with our writers.

Certainly there is every indication that Billy has resolved his ambivalences, that somewhere (and such moments are never marked consciously) he made his own decision to play "court jester"; and even to match other jesters in being funnier than they. And somehow he came to like it, and to thrive on it, and even to build his life upon it.

The fact that, in the main, his childhood inculcation of music and creativity now carries basically *good* associations is demonstrated in his ritualistic habit of always using his old piano—"I have always known this piano"—for his composing. He has a baby grand, of which he is proud; he has an electric piano; but he has "never composed anything except on that old piano . . . I feel it's lucky and I feel at home with it."

"The tune," says Billy, "is always easy, it just comes." As he puts it, so beautifully, . . . "It is almost God-given . . . it opens something and it comes." He sticks always to a certain pattern, not really knowing if it's necessary, but feeling as though he must.

Again the deceptive nature of creativity . . . for Billy, it seems almost like a series of automatic, or involuntary responses, as though he plugged himself in! As others of our writers who are involved in television explain, you don't have time to think, to delay. Billy does from three to five songs a week. He still fears the possibility of failing. He admits honestly that he's "bombed about four times in three years," but also rationalizes realistically: "that's not bad."

So, despite his years of success, despite the adulation that has been his since he was a young child, Billy never turned into a "spoiled adult," nor does he seem to operate p 'marily out of the need for external reinforcement. Ra.   · it is clear that it is his nature to create, and that his own combination of humor and music is —symbolized by his speech and motor patterns—uniquely *him.*

Billy Barnes is a twentieth-century jester who can serve as his own Muse. His rhythm is the patter of contemporary existence, fast-paced, abundant with stimuli. His lyrics synthesize, cleverly and singularly, the whirl of the wild world we have built, carrying the slim wind of a dream of transcending that world with explosions of laughter.

Arnie Rosen

Play and Paradox

ARNIE ROSEN was born in 1921 in Brooklyn. He began writing seriously in 1949. His hobbies are art collecting and reading.

When asked how he felt when he had written something he particularly liked he wrote the following: "I feel great. There's an exaltation; it relieves weariness . . . you get an idea and you suddenly see the light at the end of the tunnel. If you're successful in what you're trying to do, it's stimulating. One of the writers had a very fanciful line for the minds of comedy writers: 'they don't work, they play.' The mind doesn't work, it plays."

A partial listing of his credits is as follows: Arnie Rosen has written for Jackie Gleason, Milton Berle, the Bilko Show, the Garry Moore Show, and The Entertainers. As producer-writer he wrote "Get Smart." As producer-head writer he did the Carol Burnett Show, "Of Thee I Sing," a Don Rickles special, and the Mac Davis Show.

The interviewee of this section, Arnie Rosen, is known in the industry for being a businesslike, organization-minded fellow. As he indicates in this interview, his approach to his writing is very matter-of-fact. "I'll tell the staff we need this or that kind of sketch . . . and we'll apply ourselves to that . . . In television, personal routine is a luxury you can't afford . . . preoccupations can interfere initially, but I overcome them, or put them aside."

Although he is a very funny and talented writer, during the late 1960s Arnie Rosen became heavily committed to the production end of his business. His orientation comes through in this interview, where his responses are succinct, direct, terse, and to the point. He gives all indications of being an efficient, no-nonsense person.

And yet he—the image of system and orderliness—gives vivid expression to the power of play in his creative life. Simply enough, he states, "It relieves any weariness." This remark echoes the entertainment world's widespread recognition of the potent role play has in the process of creation. It adds testimony to the general realization throughout throughout human circles of the rejuvenating, stimulating, refreshing power of play.

Play is one of the basic forms of mammalian behavior. "Playful" spirit and episodes of play behavior are found throughout the kingdom of mammals.

One can easily illustrate play with examples from one's own observations. Two dogs are rolling and scuffling on the lawn. A group of kittens are tussling each other about or playing together in an overturned box. Three squirrels chase through the trees, mock-stalking and challenging. In the fields, one can witness horses, cows, pigs and all other varieties of domesticated mammals engaged in various playful acts.

Undomesticated mammals similarly manifest play in their repertoires. Otters, wild canines and felines, elephants, and various rodents are particularly playful. The many sorts of primates are probably the most constantly playful and most widely recognized for their play. The popular phrase "having as much fun as a barrel of monkeys" gives folk expression to that recognition.

We humans are the most playful of all. Play of one type or another is found at all stages of human life and throughout the expanse of human activities. It has been stated by some scientists that play is reserved predominantly for juveniles. Our observations indicate that play is certainly not *exclusive* to immature animals, and this is most conspicuously the case with humans.

Animal play generally symbolizes in fairly direct fashion some survival behavior, and is a metaphor for fighting, chasing, challenging, threating, etc.

"Metaphor" is used here in the sense designated by Gregory Bateson in his classic essay, *The Message "This is Play."* Bateson defined play as that behavior which consists of "unit actions or signals similar to but not the same as those of the behavior it resembles"—such as fighting, chasing, challenging, etc. In other words, the play sequences have close resemblance to, say, fighting, but it is quite clear to participants and usually to any audience that fighting is not taking place. If the play pact breaks down and actual fighting develops, the previous non-fighting nature of the play becomes that much more conspicuous in contrast.

Whereas animal play presents direct and simple symbolization, human play can be extremely complex, indirect, sophisticated, and subtle. The play of children tends to be more direct, similar to the play of animals. Much adult human play is of this simple nature, as with teasing, rough-house, "funning," the play of couples in love. However, the majority of human *adult* play is in the form of intellectual, verbal conduct—common examples of which are witty repartee, flirtation, various adult games such as chess or charades, organized sports, much business or political or marital maneuvering, and institutionalized play such as the theater.

The simple, direct nature of children's play allows for easy recognition. Greater complexity and subtlety of adult play give it a lower profile. The adult world is not customarily portrayed as presenting a playful mien. But this is an inaccuracy of omission. The *spirit* of play, if not its actual form, is the foundation for an easy majority of the adult's daily experiences. It is the yeast that makes palatable the daily bread.

Philosopher Johan Huizinga suggested the appellation *Homo Sapiens* be replaced by *Homo Ludens* to indicate the importance of play as "a distinct and highly important factor in the world's life and doing" . . . "civilization arises and unfolds in and as play." Perhaps the Shakespearean "all the world's a stage and all men and women merely players" is an exaggeration, and Transactional Analysis' "games people play" is simplistic. But *Homo Ludens* has a great deal to recommend it. Play is a large portion of life and, as Huizinga relates, is melded with much that is the best of life.

Innumerable creative people—artists, writers, performers, philosophers, etc.—have proclaimed the special role that play has had in the generation of their contributions to the knowledge, wisdom and/or beauty of the human experience. Whereas most of these testimonials have been impressionistic outpouring of unstructured personal enthusiasm, there is no mistaking the sincere introspection of these appraisals. Psychologist D. E. Berlyne adds valuable rigor to these appraisals with his theory of "intrinsic motivation," pointing out the commonality of intrinsic motivation to play, creativity, exploration, and esthetic enjoyment.

Play has an incalculable importance in its own right. But it has a further importance that is significantly related to the subject of this book and the product of these comedy writers' efforts—humor. There is an intimate relationship between play and humor. Play is not just valuable to humor; it is essential. Humor depends, for its being, on the mysterious, tricky structure of play. Humor goes beyond play in several important ways, but must have the mood of play to catalyze it and the structure of play to sustain it.

Humor is to play as adult is to child; as maturity is to callowness. It shares much with play, but has its own tricks and secrets. One of these is the powerful element of the punchline, which is found in humor but not in play. Play is fluid and ongoing, with no specific part standing out as a climax to the behavior, as a goal, one might say, of the interaction, or a culmination or a dénouement. On the other hand, humor is distinguished by this feature. A sharp differentiation is recognized. When Arnie Rosen speaks of comedy writers playing as they create, there is no mistake that, while they are playing, it is humor they create, *not* play.

Humor does not exist without a punchline of some sort, even in the most extreme case of captionless cartoons, where the punchline is of a visual nature, usually consisting of a graphic distortion or alteration of what is expected. One produced by Whitney Darrow, Jr., pictures a group at an art show opening. The adults stand around drinking and talking, completely ignoring the paintings. It is the infant in one woman's papoose-sling who is carefully and appreciatively examining the art work. Another extreme case is the "shaggy dog" story which rambles on and on. Even here one finds a punchline, when some comment finally precipitates a realization of the ridiculousness of all that has preceded. Many scholars have studied the punchline and expounded their views. Punchlines are described as incongruous, unexpected, a switch of ideas, a shift, a leap, a transfer, an alteration. In his volume, *The Act of Creation*, philosopher Arthur Koestler writes of the punchline as a sudden perception "of a situation or idea in two self-consistent but habitually incompatible frames of reference."

Research by one of us (Fry) has examined the psychological structure of the punchline. What emerged from that research is a schema wherein an item of humor is recognized as a double entity, consisting of both explicit content—joke, cartoon, humorous remark, etc.—and that content which is implicit. This implicit content takes form in the mind as automatic association to the explicit material, and may be either conscious or unconscious in nature. The implicit themes are as integral a part of the joke as is the explicit. Many themes are stimulated in a listener's mind by the content of a joke. The range is limited only by the breadth of individual imagination and experience.

The punchline acts to reveal a hidden truth. It reveals the association of explicit content and its implicit partners. It causes to occur an abrupt transformation of some part of that implicit content into explicit form. The previous reality of word or deed is suddenly replaced by another reality which, until the punchline, was an unreal fantasy in the listener's mind. Shade replaces substance and, in replacing, becomes substance itself.

It is at this part of humor—the punchline—that the greatest opportunity for artistry occurs. The most artistic humor presents punchlines bringing forth into reality the most unexpected, or surprising, theme. The mirth stimulated by the "best" jokes is thus accompanied by a strong sense of discovery. The finest punchlines accomplish this intellectual and emotional miracle with a minimum of effort, a brevity of words, a swiftness and smoothness of action.

Another form of artistry takes place at the moment of punchline dénouement. This is an unusual and complex artistry more easily experienced than explained. At the moment when implicit fantasy replaces explicit reality and becomes itself the reality of the moment, a *paradox* is precipitated. There is much evidence that indicates the mirth stimulated by humor does not result only from the revelation of humor's "hidden truth," and the audience's "discovery," but also from the experiencing of paradox.

Paradox is generally defined as a "statement or concept or phenomenon which is contrary to received opinion or perception, which may be self-contradictory, and which may appear to be absurd or unreasonable." It is a very particular form of paradox which is precipitated by humor's punchline. That form is known as Logical Type.

These paradoxes are self-contradictory, being self-reflexive or self-referent. The most famous of these paradoxes is that established by the ancient riddle involving the statement by the Cretan philosopher Epimenedes: "All Cretans are liars." The paradox revolves around the unsolvable question of whether the Cretan philosopher is lying, as he indicates, or whether he is telling the truth. If he is telling the truth, he is lying. If he is lying, he is telling the truth. This paradox cannot be solved, as it refers back to itself and produces an eternal circling of logic. (The interested reader is referred to a more extensive discussion of these paradoxes in the book *Sweet Madness: A Study of Humor* by Dr. Fry.)

The paradox precipitated by punchlines of humor is of this same self-reflexive type. Until the punchline is delivered, all understood reality is of the explicit content of the humorous episode. The punchline is delivered, and "reality" is suddenly found to be what was previously unreal—an implicit association to the explicit humor content. "This is unreal" becomes a statement about that moment in time; it refers back onto itself; and paradox takes place.

Already a complex phenomenon because of this punchline paradox, humor is made even more complex by being encapsulated within another "this is unreal" self-reflexive paradox. This broader, engulfing paradox reflects the intimate, essential relationship between humor and play.

Play is itself characterized by a "this is unreal" paradox. Almost anyone at almost any time can distinguish whether a creature is playing or "really means it." Something in the behavior communicates a "this is unreal" message—"I am only kidding," "we are not really fighting," "I am not actually trying to steal your bone." The agreement that "this is unreal" establishes a *play-frame*, indicating that playful behavior is framed within the context of this paradoxical designation.

Humor is also framed within play context. Humor is encapsulated within the same general "this is unreal" play-frame as is play. Many possible mechanisms can establish the humor play-frame—including "let me tell you a joke," facial expressions, a smile or a wink, dialect, posture or movement variations such as the Groucho Marx slink. All communicate that the episode is not to be taken seriously; it is a joke.

Unlike play which is without the punchline paradox, humor exhibits both play-frame paradox and punchline paradox. The amazing complexity of humor is derived, in no small measure, from the interrelationship of these two paradoxes. They are *self*-reflexive, but they also modify each other. The consequence of that interaction is the crystallization, at the moment of punchline, of an infinite set of levels of abstraction. It is as if someone suddenly kicked a hole in the heavens, and everything started to pour in, and out, at the same instant. The universe of conceived reality is temporarily suspended; and we break out into laughter.

The "this is unreal" paradox characterizes several other stimulating elements of life. Some of these are fantasy, drama, metaphoric poetry, story-telling, art. Failure to recognize a play-frame if one is having a bad dream can cause one to experience that night terror called "nightmare." A play-frame, with its attendant paradox, is also essential when one daydreams. Different forms of psychological pathology occur if the play-frame of the reverie is not conceived.

The presence of paradox-precipitating "this is unreal" as a crucial element of such widespread and important human experiences as humor and play; the operation of this frame in a large variety of other valuable human activities; the powerful role it has in the lives of other mammals through its survival value in their play behavior: these, and other considerations, suggest that the "this is unreal" phenomenon with its paradoxes has an impact far beyond that of being only an obscure philosophic oddity.

By definition, a paradox is something which surpasses present understanding. Over the centuries of recorded history, different kinds of paradoxes have been discovered, or invented, and some have been resolved. Simply, those paradoxes which have been solved are no longer paradoxes. In the case of the Logical Type self-reflexive paradoxes, solution is not yet apparent. New examples of this paradox are invented from time to time. A recent one was presented by the late artist Pablo Picasso when asked about the authenticity of a painting attributed to him. Picasso answered paradoxically, "I often paint fakes."

One is forced to conclude that these paradoxes are paradoxes because our mental equipment is not yet advanced to the stage where we can find resolution of these brain twisters. It is reasonable to conclude that paradoxes are markers on the frontier edge of human intellectual development. And paradoxes will continue to be paradoxical until the brain template has undergone the evolution necessary for their resolution.

It is impossible to predict the characteristics and consequences of that evolutionary advance. However, since these paradoxes are so intimately involved with our perception of "real" and "unreal," it is logical to assume that advance will result in a radical alteration of the human perception of reality, that our customary dichotomous differentiation between "reality" and "unreality" will be extensively modified. We can expect that some monumental changes will take place in our dreams, in our play, in our sense of humor, in our whole symbolic process. Until that time, we will continue to be entertained by the talent of persons such as Arnie Rosen.

Interview

Fry: Now, how did you get started in this business?
Rosen: I've been writing comedy since I was a kid in high school, twelve years old or so, and all throughout my life. I think once you decide on something like that, it becomes a part of you. I don't want to glorify the profession, but it's like somebody deciding to be a doctor very early and

having the luxury of knowing what he's going to do with
his life. I was born in New York—Brooklyn—which usually gets a laugh. Unless you were born there. It seems to
help if you come from the East coast and you're Jewish.
That would be a study in itself, I imagine.

Allen: Was there humor in your early life at home?

R: Not really. I had two brothers. I was the *middle*
brother of three, I'm sure that is significant in itself. I don't
remember my family as being particularly humorous.

F: Living in the house were. . .?

R: My mother, my father, and the three brothers.
Neither of my parents were born in this country. They
came here during the Great Migration with their parents.

A: And your grandparents? Did they seem particularly
humorous to you?

R: No, not really. No, they were hard-working immigrant families on both sides.

F: Well then, when something did occur in the household that was funny, what was your role?

R: Well, for me, it probably did start there, in the
family.

F: Were you the family comedian?

R: Oh, yes.

A: Do you remember any situations or certain settings
in which you acted that role—at the dinner table, for
instance? Or were you always on?

R: I don't remember. I don't have that kind of recall. I
have very often used humor in anxiety situations. I've
noticed that most comedy writers do that, in life-
situations.

F: Can you remember anything about your *style* in
those days? Was it slapstick, or did you come up with
good lines, or—

R: I dimly recall that it was more slapstick, teasing
impressions, clowning around. I would assume that the
sophistication came as I got older, when I decided I
wanted to be a writer. I excelled in putting words together,
and I found out very quickly that I was better in the lighter
aspect of it.

F: How did you find that out?

R: It was really a matter of trial and error. And then, somewhere around 12, 13, 14, I wrote a humor column for my high school newspaper.

F: How did your parents act toward the column?

R: I remember a lot of approval coming from my mother in particular, because she fancies herself, not a writer, but a *literate* person. She was an omniverous reader, and gave a great deal of approval to the things I wrote.

And so did the teacher, classmates, the neighborhood. There is always a funny person in every gang and later he becomes the comic. Every block has its Jerry Lewis. Usually, it is a kid who isn't a good athlete. That is his way of getting attention or respect.

A: Were you that person?

R: I remember that. I was. I think that it is an important part of the development of humor, as a writer or performer, to learn you've got a good gift or talent, a *flare* and it commands respect. You use it just as somebody would hit home-runs.

F: Were there any particular people who influenced you at all in the further development of this talent—a teacher, a special friend, anyone you can think of?

R: No, I really don't remember any influence like that.

A: Can you remember whether or not you admired any particular performer, or style of comedy? Was there anyone you were trying to emulate?

R: Nobody in particular. But I remember admiring certain early radio comics, tuning in to the radio; Bob Hope and Jack Benny, Fibber McGee and Molly were favorites. I realized this was the way I was going, so maybe I'd better study them.

F: Oh, you actually studied them at that early an age. What were you looking for?

R: I was absorbing—I was enjoying just listening and I considered them contemporaries, I'd consider that Bob Hope and I were both in the same business, so I'd pay him that respect, as much as you'd read an important paper by another doctor.

A: Great, how you felt the relationship already.

R: But also shows you how egocentric, how conceited I must have been.

A: At this point in your growing up, when you began to connect with what you would choose for a career, what reaction did your mother have? Did you, by the way, ever actually tell her you planned on becoming a comedy writer?

R: I don't know if I used the term "comedy writer" at that time, even though I think in retrospect I probably dreamed of it. I thought I'd be a writer, a journalist, or something like that. I didn't know I'd specialize in comedy writing. That's a realization I came to a little later.

A: Were your parents fairly amenable to this?

R: Absolutely. You see, we had no doctor-lawyer tradition in our family. I wasn't expected to follow in anybody's footsteps. I went right on ahead with it, and became the editor of my college humor magazine. Later, while I was in the Marine Corps, during lulls in the action, I wrote and produced shows. After I got out of the Service, I did about fifteen or twenty sample radio shows, using them to try to break into the business professionally. I finally did and I've been involved in it ever since.

A: What was your first professional job?

R: The Robert Q. Lewis show in New York, in 1948, five scripts—five days a week. From there I went on to Jackie Gleason, Phil Silvers, Gary Moore. I produced *Get Smart* for a year. I met Carol Burnett on the Gary Moore show, and I've done this show since its inception.

A: Can you describe a typical day of production on the show? You work as a team, right?

R: Mostly, yes. We back into it—our routine is to get together in the morning—we come in around ten o'clock, we have coffee, make preliminary phone-calls, do as many things as possible to delay getting down to business. Generally we're right here in my office, either all of us, or together in different smaller combinations, in smaller groups. I'll tell the staff we need this or that kind of sketch or an idea for a certain sketch and we'll apply ourselves to that. We have a session in which we all pitch ideas, most of which we reject amongst ourselves, fastening onto the good ones, and developing them. In other words, after accepting a *premise*, we explore it, develop it, and so on.

A: So your group goes over things, rejecting, screening out material, rewriting line by line.

R: Well, really, no. Not at that point. We are just finding out *generally* what's funny, what a situation is worth, if there is anything funny enough to continue with it. After that, I'll give out specific assignments. If one writer from a particular team has an affinity for a certain skit, I'll say, "You do a draft on that one."

F: Can you give us some examples of the kind of affinity you mean?

R: Well, there are some writers who are better *joke* writers than others, so if there is a sketch that clearly calls for several jokes, loosely linked together, we use him. Other guys are better constructionists, so they'll get a sketch with more interplay among the characters. There are some writers who do great pantomime material, where others may be more verbal. You try to give out the assignments to tap the particular strengths available. This is a good thing about writing in teams. It's also especially good for breaking up the blocks, the dry periods.

F: Can you tell us some more about that, how you personally break through a block?

R: Well, it's mostly this group situation. It's something that I encourage in all our writers. Whether they're working alone, or in teams, to never indulge themselves in that dry period or be stopped too long by that block. In a group-session, we bypass it—the stimulus of the entire group helps them over it.

A: A kind of therapy—

R: It *is*. And it invariably works.

F: You haven't always worked in a group though. You mentioned writing in the Marines and the original column.

R: I've worked alone, but I've worked for many years with a partner, and I've worked in groups.

F: What creative routines do you have while working alone?

R: I don't really remember. In television, personal routine is a luxury that you can't afford. The deadline motivates and stimulates you.

A: You've always made the deadline?

R: I've always made the deadline.

F: Have you had any special aids in the process of creativity—religion, any rituals; do you wear a special suit of clothes, use a particular typewriter?

R: No, no superstitutions.

A: Nothing at all?

R: No, well, late in the session, you know, we use coffee. Or in a crisis, something stronger. It gets done.

A: Do you have any trouble at all on occasions —outside things, distractions, bothering you when you come in to work with the other guys?

R: Yes, distractions, preoccupations can interfere initially, but I overcome them, or put them aside. This works better in a group than alone—where your problems weigh more heavily. I think this is why many writers work in teams.

A: It must be a secure feeling when you guys are together, if one of you is dry for the moment, maybe someone else isn't—

R: Right; and getting a reaction from someone else is important in itself. You can't decide whether a piece is funny or not. If it gets the other guy, you have a better idea.

F: How do you go about choosing people to work with?

R: I like to read the things they've written, I like to talk with them and see if there is a chemistry, the spark for a real relationship, if we respond to one another.

A: You've got a pretty compatible group?

R: We try—we're not always accurate, we may make mistakes, but we try for the accuracy. There's a lot of coming and going. If you find somebody compatible, you tend to hold onto them and replace those you don't care for as well, or who don't come up to what you think are your standards.

F: When writing alone, are you here, or at home?

R: Well, I write here whenever possible. Wearing two hats is very difficult for me. There are constant interruptions—the other writers, the telephone, production problems. So, I tend to write late at night, after the children are asleep and I have quiet. I have a little office off the bedroom where I work and am not disturbed by anyone else.

A: Do you think you could ever put down the rules of the trade?

R: I wouldn't even attempt it. You could write books on that. What would be applicable to one writer and one situation wouldn't be for another. I don't think there are any rules. I think comedy writing is a *state of mind*. It develops over the years. I don't think you can ever teach anybody to be a comedy writer unless he has a basic flare for it.

A: What do you feel about your own "flare?" How do you feel when you know you've just done something really good?

R: I feel great. There's an exaltation. It relieves any weariness. I've felt tired and droopy, not able to lick a particular problem, and then you feel the adrenalin pumping when you get an idea and you suddenly see the light. If you're successful in what you're trying to do, it's stimulating. One of the writers even had a very fanciful line for the minds of comedy writers. He said, they don't work, they *play*. The mind doesn't work, it plays.

Summary

"Were you the family comedian?"

"Oh, yes . . . I recall that (my style) was more slapstick, teasing impressions, clowning around. I would assume that the sophistication came as I got older."

This is the way Arnie Rosen describes the beginning of his career as a very successful and very productive comedy writer. He, like the other talented writers interviewed in this study, has contributed to the entertainment and amusement of millions of people. He and his colleagues send laughter ringing around the world.

Arnie's style of presenting himself in our interview was consistent with the description he gave of his general work and creation style. He is direct to the point of terseness, matter-of-fact, explicit. His responses to questions or suggestions were relatively brief, but pithy. He did not elaborate much, except when talking about his working relationships with his comedy team, and at those times he displayed an enthusiasm nearly verbose.

The consistent picture of Arnie which emerges from what he says about himself, his manner of conducting himself in an interview, and his general industry reputation, is completely compatible with his description of his family life-style heritage. The family itself was not particularly humorous; there was a "hard-working" tradition. The family seems to have accepted Arnie's comedy-writing orientation in a perfectly pragmatic, matter-of-fact fashion.

However, Arnie was the family comedian; he was the neighborhood comedian. "There is always a funny person in every gang—I was (that person) . . . and I've been writing comedy since I was a kid in high school, twelve years or so." His beginning style was in the clowning vein.

It would seem paradoxical that this efficient, got-it-all-together, sophisticated fellow, with his polished capability to contribute to the entertainment of the world audience, with his pragmatic and hard-working background, could ever have been a rollicking, joke-playing, slapstick clown. It is as if we discovered that the king had started out as a jester.

Despite Arnie's briefness and succinctness, he does cover a lot of territory in the interview. We can read into his comments many of the themes expressed by other comedy writers in this study. There is considerable material on the matter of internal-external reinforcement and on the singular-man multiple-man dichotomy. He offers valuable commentary on the process of creation—revealing by his interpretative responses, that he has done a good piece of deliberate thinking on the subject. And there is valuable information of other sorts, as well as the chance to get a glimpse of what must be a very exciting and pleasurable life.

However, we found that our thoughts kept returning, when considering the results of this interview, to that conflicting picture of the clown in mufti. We can accept Arnie's self-description, "I excelled in putting words together . . . it is an important part of the development of humor . . . to learn you've got a good gift or talent; a flare." We can also turn to the list of his credits, or we can observe the general upward, success-after-success course of his career. In whatever facts we place our faith, the metal rings true. He has comedic talent. The clown lives on.

And yet, as we've said, he comes across so consistently businesslike that the two images, drawn in this simplistic fashion, seem incompatible. One would, at least, expect a flashing back and forth of different elements of these two identities; a kaleidoscope of personality traits. There is no suggestion of this sort of psychic amorphism. Arnie Rosen gives strong testimony of being consistent within himself. "Preoccupations can interfere initially, but I overcome them, or put them aside." That kind of effectiveness requires internal unity.

Nor is there any evidence in Arnie of the frustration that could result from one personality style taking a dominant position and oppressively thwarting any participation or self-expression from another style. He may efficiently "put aside" distractions, but he also is able to feel great after having created something great. "If you're successful in what you're trying to do, it's stimulating." He even solves, without conflict or distress, the practical problems created by the external reality conflict caused by his double responsibility of being both comedy writer and producer. "I tend to write late at night . . . I have a little office off the bedroom where I work and am not disturbed by anyone else."

So, here we seem to have a paradox—an individual who is serious about humor. Well, it may come as a shock to discover that all these comedy writers are serious about their humor. They all have deep senses of responsibility regarding their creations; have strong respect for humor and its traditions. They don't agree on everything regarding humor. They see humor coming from different sources within the individual—Arnie believes a "basic flare" is needed. They manifest different customs of creating. But they are *unanimous* in a belief that humor is one of the most important parts of life.

There are quite a few of us who hold the same belief and share the same respect for humor. It may not be a paradox, after all, that one can be serious about comedy. It may be just a matter of perspective. The protean nature of humor should be able to handle the various attitudes with which it is approached. One should be able to be serious about humor, without humor melting away or shriveling. That protean nature accomodates to numerous different roles chosen for humor in human relationships. The comic spirit has even survived, over the centuries, the many occasions in which it has been dragged into hostile interaction.

In considering the issue of perspective as a method of understanding the paradox seemingly generated by a person being serious about humor, we are reminded of popular lore surrounding clowns and jesters. These traditional creators and presenters of comedy are conventionally depicted as figures of tragedy. "Laugh, clown, laugh": The broken heart of the clown is a symbol of widespread legend. Pagliacci's agony has brought forth the tears of millions.

In truth, most clowns are not tragic figures. They are hard working professionals who also enjoy their lives. Professional clown Tim Torkildson once stated, "I love it . . . it takes lots of discipline. But that wonderful feeling when those waves of laughter roll down!" His colleague,

Steve Smith, echoes those sentiments. "It's practice, practice, practice. It's hard work—and it's wonderful." Such opinions as these are not incompatible with the image of hard-working, efficient, skillful Arnie Rosen creating rich humor and enjoying it immensely.

One wonders how such traditions as the tragic clown get established. In this case, the explanation may well be that a simple answer was offered for a complex question, following the principle of humanity's proclivity to be taken in by the promise of an "easy way." The complex question is one personified in Arnie Rosen: "How can the man produce humor in a serious way?" The attempt at providing the simple answer states, "He's really a tragic figure underneath his outer calm. His humor is a cover-up." Clown Torkildson said, "People think clowns hide behind their make-up . . . that they are suffering a personal tragedy and hiding it with buffoonery." Again—the truth is that it isn't that simple.

As an ultimate validation of humor's protean nature and its multifarious capacity for being adapted to different human needs, we can quote Arnie Rosen's statement that, along with so many other experiences with humor, he has also used it as a cover-up. "I have often used humor in anxiety situations. I've noticed that most comedy writers do that."

And so they can and, indeed, *do* sometimes use humor in that way. But we have the testimony of these professionals that humor is much, much more to them.

One of the great contributions of Sigmund Freud was his ability to synthesize the work of others from all disciplines and ages. He was also able to discover methods for studying or reaching the unconscious. Early on, he utilized hypnosis; later, he conceived of the value of free association and, ultimately, he felt that dreams were the "royal road to the unconscious."

Since Herbie Baker feels strongly that at least some of his ideas come to him in sleep, it will be well to examine dreams here. Today, dreams are a central focus for study which has led to great advances in brain research. But what we know of dreams is not complete, although we know far more than we did only a few years ago. We know that we all dream, but many of us do not remember our dreams because we do not awaken during or close enough to the so-called REM period (rapid eye movement which takes place as we dream). We know that sleep during the REM period appears fitful. The sleeper may thrash about more at those periods of the night. This fitfulness is strange because studies have demonstrated clearly the human need for REM sleep. Subjects deprived of it often suffer from listlessness, irritability, and extreme tension on days following the deprivation. We also know that subjects awakened during REM or immediately thereafter will be capable of reporting dreams in tremendous detail. Thus, Herbie Baker would be wise to keep a pad and flashlight near his bed, for later memories of dreams are never so clear as they are when an individual first awakens.

Freud felt that dreams contained both manifest content and latent content. Although the manifest content might appear from the front of the subconscious, Freud felt that behind it there lay yet another area. In order to reach it, the dreamer must freely associate from the manifest content. According to Freud, attempts to find meaningful and cohesive stories from the manifest content alone are fruitless.

Contrary to public conceptions, Freud also recognized the individual nature of symbol systems, though he did feel there are certain universal symbols. In the main, however, the dreamer alone has the key to unlocking the meaning of his own dreams.

Freud's pupil and friend, Carl Jung concurred with him. The key to interpretation of dreams is not to be found in the skill of the therapist. Jung wrote, "I have made it a rule to remind myself that I can never understand someone else's dream well enough to interpret it correctly . . . it is essential for *him* (Authors' italics) to explore the content of a dream with the utmost thoroughness."

He conceived of the idea of the *collective unconscious* which contains common universal symbols. He felt that this realm of archetypes is represented by primeval dreams (of ancient cultures, religions, myths) and creative fantasies. Much of the material of the artist, according to Jung, is a product of the creative material which emerges from the collective unconscious.

But in the act of creating, there is no awareness of distinction between a symbol and reality—no split-second realization that the "solution" to a creative dilemma has just emerged from subconscious processes. Sometimes, there is such an abrupt eruption of the right phrase, that missing idea, that ingenious rhythm, that it may seem as though magic is taking place. And as a result of having many such incidents, the creator may come to believe that he actually has magic, or special powers. His gift of creativity, or his ability to make clever associations, may seem to him so unique that it is psychic, or that it transcends the natural.

Herbie Baker

*The Royal Road
to the Unconscious*

HERBIE BAKER was born in New York in 1920. He got his start writing comedy when he was at Yale. He has no creative hobbies, adding, "I get paid for all my hobbies." The following paragraph accompanied the snapshot we asked him for.

"The enclosed photograph was taken of me in action—in my office when I was doing the Flip Wilson Show—under ideal writing conditions. Notice the type-writer in easy typing distance, the huge stack of blank paper, the cup of coffee. Note, too, the little square sheet of paper tacked to the wall. It contains the emergency tele-phone numbers absolutely essential to any professional writer of comedy: home, the library, the psychoanalyst, and airline reservations."

As a writer he won an Emmy for "An Evening with Fred Astaire," and a Writers Guild award for "Norman Rockwell's America." He has been head writer of the Flip Wilson Show, the Danny Kaye Show, the Perry Como Show, and Gladys Knight and the Pips as well as many other specials, screenplays, and special material.

In recent years, more and more attention has been devoted to exploration of consciousness and "expanding its limits." Of course, it is not the peripheries of consciousness that are expanding, but rather the attitude of the contemporary world that is expanding. Only within the last few years have such areas as psychic healing, ESP, and altered states of consciousness (such as meditation) been considered appropriate material for serious discussion. It is true today that several outstanding researchers and authors give credence to what was considered charlatanism just a few years ago.

These subjects are of vital interest to our study of humor and the creative process, since we are dealing with (1) the ability to associate; (2) the ability to select materials out of the "apperceptive mass" within our own systems; (3) the seeming magic with which leaps to insight, discovery, and invention often occur, particularly in the humorist, who is the archetypal image of man delving quickly into the subconscious for consciously-utilized materials.

All of these discussions are highly relevant to the motif of this chapter, which was triggered by our interview with Herbie Baker. Herbie, who is serious and jolly simultaneously, firmly believes that psychic events which have occurred in his own life have sparked and sustained and earmarked his own creative style. He is a highly educated and sophisticated man who utilized much of our interview time inquiring of us as to whether or not we could scientifically support the validity of such phenomena. We could not give definitive answers to Herbie, but we are going to devote this space to some considerations to the background of the elusive concept of consciousness, dreams, symbols and what can go on when the magical moment of inspiration takes place.

Most people give Freud credit for "discovery" of the unconscious. This is inaccurate. The concept of other realms of consciousness existed in the ancient world. Such scientists as Leibnitz and Herbart were early contributors to Psychology when it was being "built" as a science separate from its parent, philosophy. Leibnitz classified mental events according to their degree of clearness, ranging from those most definitively conscious to those that seemed blurred or vague. This was the first presence of a concept widely accepted today—that we may be totally unaware of some of our thoughts; that much may linger below the surface.

Herbart outlined a real theory of the unconscious. He felt that ideas struggled against one another for their place in our consciousness. He felt that certain ideas are incapable of combining with one another and therefore, some of those ideas plop into the unconscious. Ideas are active forces—they have energy, and in order to enter consciousness, they must have enough force (and be subjected to little enough conflict with other ideas) to pass a certain threshold.

Preceding Freud's work was William James, who, in his marvelous *Principles of Psychology* described his thesis that consciousness is a continuous flow, a stream, and no one element can be separate from another. This concept of a stream of consciousness is vital to contemporary psychology and served as an extreme contrast to the prominent German laboratory psychologists who, for years, had been searching for the basic "elements of consciousness" as though they were atoms, clearly separable from one another. James was the first prominent psychologist to show interest in psychic research, by the way. Fascinated with spirituality and unexplored domains of human existence, he wrote *Varieties of Religious Experience*, a book so ahead of its time it could itself appear to be an example of clairvoyance.

(In these comments, we are not attempting to offer a rational explanation of all psychic phenomena at all.

Rather we present our perceptions of one segment of the psyche spectrum—that segment having to do with the role of the unconscious in creative experience, with perhaps the contributions made by psychic phenomena to creativity, through the unconscious. There must be many ways in which psychic phenomena can be envisioned, and we are not prepared to argue, in the context of this book, with any of them.)

These feelings frequently occur to the creator when he is in the singular-man state referred to in the Jack Elinson section of this book. While in that state and engaged in trying to create, he may experience ecstasy at the birth of the creative product and may quickly (sometimes without even being aware of it) turn to another person to share the soaring feeling he has. Particularly with a performing-creator, he is looking to the other person for assurance that his ecstasy is real. The creator knows his power at these moments and, in turning to another, is emphasizing it. In essence, he is saying, "Look, I can entertain you. *I* can make magic and that magic will make you laugh or cry or whatever *I* want it to do." Like the ancient tribal witch doctors, or the gurus or shaman, he is demonstrating himself in heroic status. He may be showing his power, declaring his uniqueness —certainly he is exhibiting his work and the special manner in which it was created.

Perhaps there is a twofold message in a writer's saying, "I got the greatest idea in a dream last night. It's just what I needed for the next show."

Despite the success or the reinforcement given a writer, he or she will experience moments of self-doubt. This has been described by all of our humor writers who wonder repeatedly if "they can do it again." They ask themselves, when blocked, talking to their most secret inner selves: "Will I be as funny the next time? In fact, can I think of anything funny at all? Maybe this time, nothing will come."

The writer is isolated and afraid; there is a black feeling of the void. There may be terrible moments of self-desecration when the writer sits at his typewriter, feeling as though the world is now about to find out the awful truth about him—that, in fact, he isn't really talented or special at all. He may say to himself at that moment that he must wait for the Muse to arrive; that he is empty inside; has nothing to give. When the words do come, the writer sometimes feels they come from some external or supernatural force. He may not really be in touch with the fact that, no matter how long it takes, it is *he* who has broken the block. His "magic show" to his audience may be for the purpose of convincing them, but above all, to convince himself that he "still has the gift."

The need to be special, and the terrible shifting between feelings of confidence and feelings of doubt haunt all of us as human beings. They surely haunt the writer who often feels that, unless he is both productive and stellar in his productivity, his very identity will disappear. Many passages in our interviews clearly show this.

Ross and Tom is the *biographie-en-deux* of two young writers who died at the peak of early success. Ross Lockridge's death was a definite suicide, immediate upon the publication of his masterpiece, *Raintree County*. The death of Thomas Heggen (*Mr. Roberts*) in the bathtub and termed accidental, but it is well-known that he was in despair at that time. Both had received numerous accolades and prizes. For neither of them was that enough. Both deeply feared that they would eventually be judged inferior.

So, in situations like this, a writer is not saying, "A funny thing happened to me on the way to the theater," but rather, "I sure hope something happens to me on the way to the theater, and that it's funny!"

In this chapter, Herbie Baker muses over his own ESP experiences, his own experiences with telepathy, wherein he feels that events have been transmitted to him in dreams or outside known sensory channels while in a waking state. For instance, he guessed that Mrs. Fry's name was Elizabeth, and was very proud of this fact.

The relationship between Herbie's writing and this facet of his existence seems an integral one. You may ask yourself, while reading his interview, what part you think this plays in Herbie's judgment of his own talent and in his normal social role.

Interview

Allen: How did you get started in humor?

Baker: I was born into it. My mother, Belle Baker, was a very big hit in vaudeville, and at that time, she was playing the Palace Theater. It was the shrine, the Mecca of all vaudeville, and she was supposedly in her seventh month. She sang a song, very fast, called "Yiddisha Momma" and the ending was on a very high note . . . "to my wonderful Yiddisha MOM." Well, when she hit the "MOM," I turned over in her, and she went right down on the stage. The curtain fell; they rushed her to the hospital; and in twenty minutes I was born. I was *really* practically born on the stage of the Palace Theater.

I've been around performers from the day I was born. When I was a kid, I'd do imitations of them. Uncle Miltie was really Uncle Miltie to me. Uncle George was George Jessel. Uncle Eddie, Eddie Cantor. Aunt Fanny was Fanny Brice. I loved doing imitations of all of them. When I was two years old, my mother brought me out on the stage. She was one of the first to bring her child out on the stage and, after that, it became very popular.

Fry: What was your role on the stage at that time?

B: I would lead the orchestra—at the age of two, I led the orchestra, and then I'd take a bow.

A: Did you enjoy it?

B: No, I don't think I really did, but I was accustomed to it. That was my function. I really didn't like it.

A: So you grew up in show business?

B: Well, on the one hand there was show business and Lindy's restaurant—the flavor of vaudeville. But on the other hand, I was given a very good formal education. I graduated *cum laude* from Tenney, which is a prep school in New Jersey, then I went on to Yale, where I was on the

Dean's list. Later, I went on for my Master's Degree. So, you see I've lived in two worlds. The two worlds did overlap somewhat in that I majored in drama at Yale, when I became an actor. Then when I was in the Army, I fell in with Godfrey Reinhardt, who was the son of Max Reinhardt, and I wound up doing the lyrics for one of his Broadway shows.

A: Had you ever written before that?

B: Not really. Oh, I had written a few things at Yale. In the Army, I was acting and directing. The world I came back into was *not* vaudeville. I didn't become a juggler. If I had become a vaudeville act, then you might say I went back to my childhood. But I didn't really.

A: Can you give us some idea how you began writing. It seems that you more or less slid into it.

B: That's the way it happened. I appeared in a play at the School for Social Research in Greenwich Village. I was very naive about a lot of things, and you know they say that God looks after drunks and fools, and occasionally very naive people. I was supposed to have all this sophistication from my show business upbringing but really I was very naive about a lot of things. I made a start as an actor.

After I met Godfrey, I wrote the lyrics for his show called "Helen Goes to Troy" with Offenbach's music, a takeoff on the Greek classic, and the biggest laugh in it was when they sang to Paris: "You say that you are Paris, King Priam's pride and joy. The last time I saw Paris, he was just a little boy." Kronenberger, *the* critic at the time, singled that out. He wrote, "I don't know whether I loved it or hated it." After that, I wrote pictures for Martin and Lewis, for Cary Grant, and I wrote the first Fred Astaire television special, which was an unusually lovely show.

F: You weren't a comedy writer from the beginning?

B: No, I haven't usually written comedies *per se*. I've done musically-oriented comedy for people like Perry Como, Dean Martin, and Danny Kaye. Flip Wilson is the first non-musical performer I've ever worked with, but I've managed, with Bob Henry's help, to make him somewhat musical.

A: Did you play an instrument when you were younger?

B: Yes, I play the piano. I also was a drummer from way back. My son is a drummer now with Bobby Gentry. He was the drummer for Janis Joplin. Before that, he drummed for Judy Collins. He's very good. He is very talented. I'm impressed with him. Oh, this is interesting. He was born on my birthday. My mother, he, and I were all born around the same time on Christmas day and we were all premature babies. Of course, we all ended up in show business. Robert Ripley printed that in "Believe it or not." Parapsychology may or may not have something to do with that.

Of course, I must have followed the lead from my mother. She was a sometime singer, sometime co-medienne, sometime singing comedienne, she sang very funny songs—like Fanny Brice, like Sophie Tucker. Irving Berlin wrote comedy material for her, but also love ballads, many of which became part of the literature of Tin Pan Alley. Songs he wrote as her special material . . . such as *How Deep is the Ocean, I'll be Loving You Always, All Alone on the Telephone, What'll I do*, etc.—All those songs were originally written for my mother.

Being around show business from my earliest days, I discovered that the majority of people in the business are Jews, and furthermore that most comedy writers are Jewish. You'll find that. It's a historical motif, and it has something to do with the Jewish personality, the Jewish ethos. The Jews laugh and they cry. They laugh, and they make other people laugh, and other people make them cry.

A: A majority of the people we've interviewed *are* Jewish. We've also found that there seem to be, among comedy-writers, a couple of predominant types. For instance, some seem to be very quiet, even withdrawn at times; While others—

B: *Yes*, there are two very distinct types. You are absolutely correct. I could name fifty brilliant comedic writers who sit quietly at a table, very quiet, withdrawn, just as you said. But there's an equal number who are the way I am. Every five minutes I'll do a routine for you, a little dance for you, you know what I mean?

F: Would you be apt to do that at a social gathering?

B: Oh, yes. I am considered to be a legitimate life of the party. I don't feel it is immodest to say that—maybe it's a sickness. I am a legitimate life of the party. They try to get me to parties because I am always the gadfly—in a nice way, you know.

A: And you have a good time while "in the act?"

B: I have a marvelous time; I *love* it! At the piano, I do songs. I can sit right down at the piano and make up songs about anyone—about you, for instance, using your name and your field of research. I have great luck with scientific people. There were two analysts at a party once. I had such fun with them—having a little sport with them.

A: What is your experience at moments like that? What kind of response do you anticipate? How do you feel?

B: It's old hat to me, I expect, by now. It's as comfortable as an old shoe. I'm having fun, but you see this kind of scene goes back to when I was three. I was always in a mob. When I'm not marvelous, I'm letting down the sides. I *expect* to be marvelous. I know this might sound terrible, but I'm telling you the truth. I expect to be good, to turn them on, and if I'm not, there is only me to blame.

A: What happens to you when you're not?

B: Thank God, it hasn't really, really happened. If it starts to get shaky, I have such ego that, well, if things aren't going particularly well, I start to laugh and make a comedy routine out of *that*. Let's say, the key is a certain *line*. If the group doesn't laugh at that, I usually stop and go into a whole new kind of routine—because I'm not going to sit there and die, I'm just not. I can always tell after a while what they'll laugh at. When they do laugh at a key line, I know I'm home. If I'm dying, I make a routine act of it.

A: You then capitalize on it?

B: Yes, absolutely.

F: Are you referring to timing? Do you learn these things?

B: You're born with it, absolutely born with a sense of timing and it is not acquired.

F: What are the rules?

B: There *are* none. You get a feeling that the timing is right. Either you have it, or you don't. It's so instinctual, it really defies analysis. Jack Benny had the greatest timing of anyone I can think of. It's not something he acquired over the years; he always had this gift. Now, it *is* true that when performers start out, their sense of timing isn't too sharp. That comes through experience—waiting for a laugh, knowing when to come in. For instance, the moment the laugh is dying—here, I think of Bob Hope—Bob Hope has this down, it's almost a mechanical thing with him. He'll tell a joke, the audience will scream. He'll know by instinct when to start telling the next one so that the last one comes down and they'll listen to the next, but the first one will still be alive. Neophytes step on their own laughs, swallow up words, you know? They don't wait long enough, or maybe they wait too long, or they wait for a laugh to die down completely then have to start building all over again. That's like lettuce. Lettuce is a metabolic food—in other words, it takes more energy to eat it than it adds to you calorically. You know, laughter can feed on itself to create more laughter, a rolling laughter. In other words—more often with physical than with verbal routines—it builds, so that you can find yourself reduced to helplessness at something going on up there on the stage or the screen. You start laughing and giggling irrepressibly at something, and it might not be all that funny. There's a sequence, a wedding night sequence. She gets her head through the wrong hole in her nightgown. And there's the groom, he's trying, you know. It's one of those French numbers. It's supposed to be sexy but she put her head through the armhole. And it's one of those things—it doesn't matter what they say, you start laughing and it builds and it builds. And that, of course, is what you always work for.

There are, of course, particular techniques you get to know, like the switch. In the switch, you take a familiar or a conventional story idea and you . . . switch it. There's a famous burlesque sketch, and a rather vulgar one, terribly funny though. A man checks into a room in a hotel. Now the lights go up on the adjoining hotel room and newlyweds come in. They have a tremendous suitcase, and they're trying to pack something into the suitcase. All right, that's the setting. Now, the bride will say—and I really don't mean to be vulgar, but it's the standard burlesque sketch—she will say something to the groom. "I don't think we can stuff it in, you'll have to stand on it." And in the next room the comic will do his take and the house will fall apart. And variations of that. I think the last line is, "If we can't, we'll just throw it out the window." Now, we are contemplating having Ruth Gordon on this show, and we do a switch on the two rooms gag.

Ruth Gordon enters one room. On the phone she says, "Hello, operator, this is Ruth Gordon. I'm opening a show tonight, and I want to go over my lines so please I must not be disturbed. I don't want the phone to ring, I don't care who it is." She hangs up. She opens the script and she begins to read. Lights up in the adjoining hotel room. Flip comes in, just checking in, he's about to put his suitcase down, or whatever, and Ruth Gordon says, "If you touch me, I'll scream." She's reading a line. "He's coming closer, closer, I've got to call the police." That is really a switch. It's based on Flip's hearing through the walls, leading him to the wrong assumption. That's an example of the switch.

You take a standard bit like this one: "Why does the chicken cross the road?" "To get to the other side." Now, the switch. "Why does the chicken cross the road?" "To get away from Colonel Sanders." The switch forms a great basis for much contemporary comedy. Nowadays we go back to old ideas. Keep all your old clothes, they'll come back in style, one way or another.

A: Do these techniques come on automatically? Or is this the kind of thing you would be apt to pull out of a hat *deliberately* because you're experienced and you know a certain bit will work in a particular situation? For instance, in the act of writing, would you be apt to say to yourself, this point calls for a switch?

B: Yes, I'd say that. At my age I probably should be a lot more quiet, a lot more cynical. I should be a lot more inured to the exigencies of the business of writing but I'm not. I'm really as I was when I started—*enthusiastic.* It's almost as though I'd never written a show, never won an award, never been paid a good salary. But, all the same, the process isn't always *physical* with me.

A: Yet you don't feel your humor is commercialized. You've learned to use what you know is going to be successful?

B: I want to tell you something about writers, particularly comedy writers. He will use any experience. He will use experiences of all human beings in this world. Even in the middle of the most passionate love affair, he might stop and say, "Hey, I just thought of a great idea for my show." He'll even use his mother if it will get him a laugh. That's true of comedians, also. They'll use their wives, their mothers, their sons, their daughters. In many ways a comedy writer or performer is a loathesome creature. Nothing is sacred to him if it will bring a laugh.

F: Are you still enthusiastic enough to watch your own shows?

B: Oh, of course, especially after the pressure of writing them. To tell you the truth, I try very hard to make the shows something I can get a kick out of. I write in a style that has been called serio-comic to make it more interesting for myself, and add another dimension to the show simultaneously. I haven't always been a television writer—so it can be very difficult. I'm leveling with you.

F: Difficult from what standpoint?

B: The pressures, the deadlines. Look, I'm here now with you and simultaneously my head is in the fact that there are several pages that must be written before I can go home tonight. And there's a meeting of the Guild I have to attend at 8:15. The show is being taped Friday and everything has to be written and reviewed and revised and rewritten in time for the taping to go smoothly on Friday.

Also next Friday's show has to be finished and the script for the Friday after that must at least be in the works by the end of the week. One has to sit on top of all of that, *I* have to sit on top of all of that, so it's a very difficult thing. And I'm so obviously "thin and frail and delicate." I should be at home, lying on my veranda, and having checks come in from people I don't even know. Anything less than that is a compromise with reality.

F: What kind of props do you use to help make reality more comfortable? Do you sit at a desk? Do you dictate into a machine, or use a secretary?

B: It varies with different writers. A friend of mine who is a very successful writer dictates for hours and gets it all out in one day. Then he culls and sharpens and dictates again. Most writers I know do not dictate. They're inhibited by microphones or even by a secretary. I'm one of those; I'm a little inhibited in those situations. I write in longhand, or sometimes do a rough on the typewriter. Then I go over it. That's how I work. I'm very fast. Maybe if I weren't so fast, I'd be a better writer. I don't know; I can't evaluate my work. There are days when I'm absolutely fantastic, and there are days when I think I get away with murder.

F: Are there certain ways you attempt to control or manage your output, your ability? What do you do when you block, for instance?

B: You cry a little. You're blocked and you really know what you've done and nothing seems right to you. Sometimes you get lucky. I believe God takes pity on me and throws me an idea.

A: Do you have any particular technique you've depended on in the past when you get into that kind of slump?

B: I wish I could be like a batter when he goes into a slump. He changes his stance or his grip on the bat. He does realistic things like stepping into the ball more. Whatever he *is* doing is not what he *was* doing. Finally somebody gets a hold of him and says, "Here's a picture of you in a hitting streak. You weren't doing any of the things you're doing now." With writers, you can't get an idea, you're blocked, everything seems trite and stale. I don't know what gets you out of it. I couldn't tell you. I wish I could.

F: Is there a particular time of day when you find you can break through a block more easily? Is it easier in the morning or do you ever wake up in the middle of the night?

B: Almost every night of the year when I go to sleep I am thinking of ideas or trying to think of an idea or pursuing an idea, and in the interim, I *dream* of an idea.

I'd like to ask *you* some questions about that. I have dreamed—and know others who have dreamed—plots, stories, ideas, that seem truly wonderful. When I wake up, I don't look out the window, because if I look out the window, I lose them. That's my superstition. With me, it's a fact. You wake up in the morning having dreamed something and if you look out the window, the chances are you won't remember what you dreamed. It's simply wonderful when you dream and you wake up and you're all excited and you think about an idea. Many times it's the most ridiculous idea you ever had, many times, not always, but many times. The mind is grabbing from all the sources it has to put together an idea.

A: Do the dreams usually come in visual or in verbal form?

B: It's always visual with me.

A: Do you actually see the people in the scenes?

B: Yes. You dream lines, too. It *can* be verbal. You dream it all.

F: When did you first become aware of this ability?

B: This isn't an ability.

F: Well, perhaps "avenue of creation" would be a better term.

B: I don't know. It's not a thing that happens a lot, but it *does* happen, and sometimes it works. I can remember it happening way back, when I was very young. Very young. And when I say young, I mean very young. I remember dreaming all the way back to when I was six months old, which I am told is very young to remember—but I'm telling you I see it in front of my eyes.

This dream I told to my mother. She was so amazed that she told me the full story behind my dream, a story she'd never told me before. In the dream, an ambulance was coming for my mother and taking her away. I saw the color of the house, the shape of the doorway, and I viewed all the circumstances in detail. She had never told me at the time because you didn't tell children such things in those days. What had happened was that soon after I was born she became pregnant again, too soon really, and had a miscarriage of some type.

Listen, I must tell you this gets us into the area of ESP. Time and time again I have stayed away from this because I didn't want to get into it. But ESP is how you sometimes unblock. I'm not jiving you. I'm telling you the truth because I know it's a scientific thing. The worst thing I could do would be to lie to you, knowingly, and I would never do that. There will be times when Bob (Henry) will call me and I'll say something to him and he'll say, "Oh, my God, we were just talking about that," or "That's exactly why I'm calling you." This sort of thing happens. The moment I think of a name I haven't thought of for years, I know I'll hear from him. I know it. Just a couple of weeks ago I happened to be chatting about a fellow named Howard Phillips, whom I haven't seen or heard from in twelve years. The next day I got a letter from him, congratulating me on winning the Emmy.

Time and time again I will come up with an idea and take up the paper the next day and find that somebody has sold that idea or it is being made into a film. If it had happened once or twice, I'd say, "Okay, it's chance, and forget it." But it happens over and over again. I've caught an idea from somewhere. I'm fascinated with this whole thing. Somehow I feel that, however you interpret it, it's what helps separate *me* from other writers who are equally experienced. You have six or seven professional writers, experienced writers, with basically the same background and experience, and you can take a situation—that situation demands ideas and the chances are that all of us will have pretty much the same comedic approach to that situation, we will all be in touch with the possible variations of that situation. When you find the fellow who thinks of something the others would have never thought of, you cover him up, he might catch a cold.

Summary

"I was *really* practically born on the stage of the Palace Theater," Herbie Baker told us early in our meeting with him. He was proudly exhibiting his credentials as a life-long member of show business—not with pretension—but with pride, and just a little anticipation of telling the terrific story surrounding his birth.

And so Herbie fascinated and charmed us with stories of his childhood and of his uncles: Miltie, Georgie, Eddie and his Aunt Fanny. Brought onto the stage at the age of two, from the beginning he held a ticket to the inner circle of the Business.

Yet, part of him split off into the quest for other credentials—academic ones. Obviously of high intelligence, Herbie nonetheless let us know he graduated cum laude from his prep school, and was on the Dean's List at Yale. He wanted us to know that, although he is *of* the Business and a success *in* the Business, he is also *above* the Business. In other words, he isn't "just another show-biz kid grown up," he is special.

Herbie went to the war, did his first writing, and came back into the theater, but not into vaudeville. One remembers Ruth Flippen's words, telling of how in her childhood and within her success, she still felt a kind of stigma from her work, despite the fact that it made her the focus of the family. Others, friends at school in particular, treated her as though she were different. In those days, it wasn't always so chic to be in show business—in vaudeville. Hence, the old sign: "No actors or dogs allowed."

Perhaps there is a fragment of this in Herbie; the memory of not being quite so proper. And perhaps this is why his mother, Belle, used her success and money to send him out of Manhattan into a prep school and later to Yale.

So, after the war, Herbie's lyrics made a hit in a Godfrey Reinhardt show. He wrote with intelligence and sophistication, but admits that, in actuality, he was very naive.

"You say that you are Paris, King Priam's pride and joy.
The last time I saw Paris, he was just a little boy."

Herbie told us that Kronenberger, *the* critic at the time, singled that line out and wrote, "I don't know whether I loved it or hated it." We got the feeling that in addition to sharing with us the cleverness of the lines, Herbie may have wanted to let us know he was reviewed by the best, and that Kronenberger's comments might be—without his knowing it—a reflection of fleeting self-doubts that he himself sometimes has.

Herbie repeatedly made allusions to psychic experience in his interview, beginning with his observation on the Christmas Day births of so many generations of his family. All of them ended up in show business. This was written up in "Believe It Or Not" several years ago. Was Herbie saying to us:

"Do you believe it or not that I come from a very special family?" If so, our answer is that we believe him. His talent is obvious; he is ingenious, even in his conversation with us. We don't know, *if* subconsciously, he also may treasure his birth on Christmas Day. This kind of mystical tie to the Christ myth has been important to many Jewish people (any who have ever experienced inferiority from their heritage).

The need *not* to be inferior is seen in Herbie's delineation of the two types of comedic writers to which we've alluded in other sections of this book. He definitely puts himself in the "performing" category, "Every five minutes I'll do a routine for you, a little dance for you, you know what I mean?" Then he proceeds to show us, through stories, that he is "a legitimate life of the party." He says that he "doesn't feel it immodest to say that," but then adds, as though in apology, "Maybe it's a sickness." Like Norman Lear, who also 'entertains' socially, he does seem to have some conflict over this part of himself, yet he "*loves* it."

Along this same line, he lets us know that he "*expects* to be marvelous." And that he capitalizes on even the bad moments to get the laughter going, "to be good."

And to be good, he (and he claims this is true for humorists in general) will use any material that seems ripe. "Nothing is sacred . . . if it will bring a laugh." In the section wherein Herbie is describing this, we make clear contact with the need of the writer-humorist to get hold of funny material. How strong this need can be, particularly when faced with the deadline-pressure! You really *feel* his stress; he loves his work, he is enthusiastic, but being in television *is* a stress.

And then the wonderful section of his interview when he discusses blocks and freely gives reinforcement for the hypotheses discussed in the beginning of this chapter. In trying to get out of the block, what does he do . . . sometimes, he says, he cries a little. Nothing seems right. And, significantly, he says this:

> Sometimes you get lucky. I believe God takes pity at me and throws me an idea.

So the entrée into that dark struggle within. The writer asks himself whether or not he holds the ticket to his own salvation, whether he is in control over his own destiny. And all of this balanced on the slim premise of the next joke, the next situation, the third skit in next Friday's show.

Here can be the importance of having that secure feeling of "resources." For Herbie, these are his telepathic experiences. His ideas come to him in dreams, rescuing him from the blocks. And he admits to the superstition that, if he even "looks out the window," the idea will be lost. He says about these periods of blocks: "The mind is grabbing from all the sources it has to put together an idea." But, reminiscent of that need to believe in magic, of which we spoke earlier, Herbie did not say: "The mind is grabbing from its greatest source—itself." It is as though ideas cannot only fly out the window; they can also fly in! This is a truly fascinating phenomenon: the creator, somehow separated from the knowledge that the dreams are his; the ideas are his. We know that Herbie intellectually knows the dreams and ideas are his, but a flicker of doubt in him allows him to share with us his questions about his own control, his own power. "ESP," says Herbie, "is how you sometimes unblock."

Indeed, this may well be true. Certainly we do not doubt any of the experiences Herbie told us about. There *is* a touch of magic to them. But the source of the magic is Herbie *himself*, in *human form*. His crisp wit and impressive intelligence express a secret that he only flirts with, that he is his own guru and that his dreams and their symbols are his own property.

We felt a great deal for this exceptional man, seeing our own reflections in his eyes. In Herbie, we experienced that dilemma of the idealist who whispers in his secret soul: "Will I ever be good enough to meet my own standards? Will anyone ever find out that I'm not as smart as they said I was when I was a kid?" And we heard in return the force of the idealist while involved in the practical world, *making something of himself, from himself:* "You may never meet your standards, because they are high, but this is a great line here. These words sound beautiful together. You have a definite gift for sound and for rhythm and for making life come to life. You're okay." So, with Herbie, did we experience again the feelings of power and of powerlessness in all of us.

Selected Readings

Ashby, W. Ross—*Design for a Brain*—John Wiley & Sons, Inc., 1952.

Bateson, Gregory—*Steps to an Ecology of Mind*—Ballantine Books, 1972.

Berlyne, D. E.—Laughter, Humor and Play—*Handbook of Social Psychology, ed. G. Lindzey & E. Aronson*—Addison Wesley, 1966.

Berger, Arthur Asa—*The Comic-Stripped American*—Walker & Co., 1973.

Chapman, Tony & Foot, Hugh—*Humour and Laughter*—John Wiley & Sons, Inc., 1975.

Fry, William F., Jr.—*Sweet Madness: A Study of Humor*—Pacific Books, 1963.

Goffman, Erving—*Frame Analysis*—Harper & Row, 1974.

Goldstein, J. H. & McGhee, P. E.—*The Psychology of Humor*—Academic Press, 1972.

Grotjahn, Martin—*Beyond Laughter*—McGraw-Hill, 1957.

Heuscher, Julius E.—*A Psychiatric Study of Myths and Fairy Tales*—C. C. Thomas, 1974.

Huizinga, Johan—*Homo Ludens*—Routledge and Kegan Paul, 1949.

Koestler, Arthur—*The Act of Creation*—The Macmillan Co., 1964.

Lorenz, Konrad—*On Aggression*—Harcourt, Brace & World, 1963.

Mindess, Harvey—*Laughter and Liberation*—Nash, 1971.

Niklaus, Thelma—*Harlequin*—George Braziller, Inc., 1956.

Nicoll, Allardyce—*The World of Harlequin*—Cambridge Univ., 1963.

Ostwald, Peter—*Soundmaking*—C. C. Thomas, 1963.

Pribram, Karl—*Languages of the Brain*—Prentice-Hall, Inc., 1971.

Shibles, Warren—*Metaphor*—The Language Press, 1971.

Spitzer, Robert—*Tidings of Comfort & Joy*—Science and Behavior Books, Inc., 1975.

van Lawick-Goodall, Jane—*In the Shadow of Man*—Houghton Mifflin, 1971.

Bugental, James F. T.—*Challenges of Humanistic Psychology* (an anthology)—Mcgraw-Hill, 1967.

Buhler, Charlotte and Allen, Melanie—*An Introduction to Humanistic Psychology*—Brooks/Cole, 1972.

Camus, Albert—*The Myth of Sisyphus and Other Essays*—Knopf, 1955.

Freud, Sigmund—Jokes and their relation to the unconscious—1905. (i.e. this was not a book)

Jung, Carl G.—*Man and His Symbols*—Doubleday, 1964.

Maslow, Abraham H.—*Toward a Psychology of Being*—Van Nostrand, 1961.

Ornstein, Robert E. (Ed.)—*The Nature of Human Consciousness* (a book of readings)—Viking, 1974.

Rotter, Julian B., Chance, June E., and Phares, E. Jerry—*Applications of a Social Learning Theory of Personality*—Holt, Rinehart & Winston, 1972.

Woods, Ralph L. & Greenhouse, Herbert B. (Eds.)—*The New World of Dreams* (an anthology)—Macmillan, 1974.

The absurdities of any one man are no greater
than those of any other man;
Humour recognizes this
and serves as the great leveler of mankind—
Laughter is a life-cry,
the spontaneous triumph of one moment
over a lifetime's absurdities.

—Melanie Allen

Pierce with a common household pin,
Many, many times,
the thickness of a black granite chunk.
Then hold that cobble up against the sun.

The secret waters in the earth will begin to flow,
the lizards sing
and jewels will tumble from the sky.
Your world will never be the same.

—William F. Fry, Jr.